PALEO
SLOW COOKING

GLUTEN FREE RECIPES MADE SIMPLE

By
Chrissy Gower

Photographs by Shannon Rosan

VICTORY BELT PUBLISHING INC.

Las Vegas

First Published in 2012 by Victory Belt Publishing Inc.

Copyright © 2012 Chrissy Gower

ISBN 13: 978-1-936608-69-0

Cover photo and recipe photos by Shannon Rosan, www.shannonrosan.com

Printed in The USA

RRD1211

PALEO
SLOW COOKING

TABLE OF CONTENTS:

Recipes:

Breakfast

Thumbnail Recipe Table of Contents

74

Bone Broth

76

Slow Cooked Chicken Stock

78

Nicki's Indian Lamb Stew

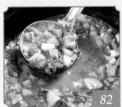
80

Chipotle Chicken Stew

82

Traditional Minestrone Soup

84

Jalapeño Sweet Potato Chowder

86

Stuenkel Stew

88

Old Fashioned Beef Stew

90

Manhattan Clam Chowder

92

Hot and Sour Soup

94

Tortilla-less Chicken Soup

96

Creamy Tomato Soup

98

Hearty Butternut Squash Soup

100

Lazy Man's Chuck Roast Stew

102

Coconut Cream of Broccoli Soup

104

Classic Chicken Soup

106

South of the Border Beef Stew

Soups and Stews

Main Dishes

Fire-Roasted Meatloaf
110

Boneless Pork Ribs
112

Spaghetti with Meat Sauce
114

Beef Brisket Sandwich
116

Mild Yellow Chicken Curry
118

Pesto Chicken
120

Slow Cooked Chili Verde
122

Mild Shredded Chicken
124

Slow Cooked Ham
126

Chicken Cacciatore
128

Sloppy Joes
130

Chili with a Kick
132

Butternut Squash Lasagna
134

Grandpa's BBQ Beef
136

Red Beef Curry
138

Aunt Robin's Roast
140

Stuffed Artichokes
142

Orange Maple Glazed Pork Chops
144

NorCal Margarita
Chicken 146

Lemon Herb Pork
Loin 148

Grandpa's Saucy
Ribs 150

Herb Rubbed
Turkey Breast 152

Slow Cooked
Buffalo Wings 154

Carne Asada 156

Chipotle Meatballs 158

Cajun Veggies
with Grilled Shrimp 160

Stuffed Acorn
Squash 162

Slow Cooked
Whole Chicken 164

Fire-Roasted Pork
Loin 166

Asian Chicken
Wraps 168

BBQ Apple Chicken 170

Chili Beef Short Ribs 172

Beef Shoulder Roast 174

Fiesta Lime Chicken 176

Bacon Bruschetta
Stuffed Chicken
Breasts 178

Main Dishes

Side Dishes

Cauliflower Rice — 182

Cauliflower Fried Rice — 184

Sautéed Kale, Onion, and Bacon — 186

Grandpa's BBQ Sauce — 188

Citrus Spinach Salad — 190

Caramelized Onion and Chard Salad — 192

Kayden's Kale Chips — 194

Roasted Brussels Sprouts — 196

Pineapple Mango Jicama Salsa — 198

Sulsa Verde — 200

Garlic Spinach — 202

Slow Cooked Sweet Potatoes — 204

Sweet Potato Chips — 206

Simple Cabbage and Cilantro Salad — 208

Grilled Asparagus — 210

Broccoli Sauté — 212

Garlic Mashed Sweet Potatoes — 214

Avocado Salsa — 216

Cucumber Salad — 218

Spaghetti Squash — 220

Robb's Post Workout Carbaganza! — 222

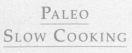

Desserts

Banana Bread

226

Tempting Chocolate Cake

228

Chocolate Almond Butter Swirl Brownies

230

Apple Crumble

232

Berry Crumble

234

Spice Blends

236

Foreword
by Robb Wolf

Author of *The New York Times* Best-Seller, *The Paleo Solution*

If you asked one hundred people what cooking method they prefer—grilling, roasting, baking, etc.—I doubt if "slow cooking" would rank near the top of the list. Why might this be? I think slow cooking is viewed as some kind of archaic, lowbrow cooking method. That's really a shame. Hopefully, Chrissy Gower's *Paleo Slow Cooking* will help change that perception.

Now, slow cooking is certainly old. In fact, it is likely one of the oldest cooking methods humans have used (300,000-500,000 years old according to some archeologists), but it is most assuredly not archaic! Slow cooking is perhaps unique amongst cooking methods in that it addresses most, if not all, of the common excuses and concerns facing the modern cook, be they a metropolitan foodie or college student who does not know which part of the can to open (hint: not the middle). Having run a gym for nearly ten years and talked with thousands of clients about food and cooking, here are some concerns that folks usually have that slow cooking addresses:

Time

Slow cooking does take a while to happen (one might get that from the name, but you never know). Unless your Internet is down, and you do not have a lawn to watch grow, you likely have better things to do than watch your slow cooker do its job. The cook time may be several hours, but preparation and actual time you need to invest in the project is on the order of ten minutes or less most of the time. You might need to plan ahead a bit—"I want to eat dinner tonight; maybe I should start the slow cooker this morning"—but if you have a pulse and anything approximating a normal EEG, you should be able to figure out how to plan ahead

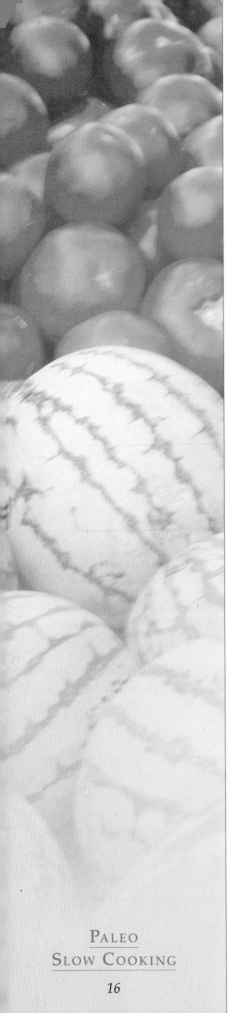

enough to launch a meal three to eight hours before you need to eat it. A side benefit of the slow cooker is that you can prep enough food to have several meals ready! Shucks, that's almost like multitasking.

Skills

Some folks legitimately do not know how to cook these days. Mom and dad did everything for them, or they have lived on frozen or fast food since getting weaned from the boob. Since this is a cookbook, I won't delve into the problems of hamstringing our kids by doing everything for them, but the problem isn't going away anytime soon. The solution is to provide folks with a foolproof method of cooking that they will love. Slow cooking is that method. Food and spices go in (Chrissy tells you exactly how much, but even if you do something wild like "experiment" it's pretty tough to mess these up), the lid goes on top, and the dial or button is toggled to "on." If that still seems outside your skill set, please consider taking the bus, as driving seems ill-advised.

Health

Many cooking methods carry health stigmas. Frying implies "fat," and everybody knows fat will kill you as surely as a bean burrito eater makes methane. Boiling removes vitamins and minerals. Grilling creates these nasty little chemical species called "polycyclic aromatic hydrocarbons," which are implicated in the damaging of DNA! Maybe we should just forego cooking and become raw-foodists! Back away from the knives and vegetable peelers, Kiddo, it does not need to be that hard.

Slow cooking is great because you have 100% control of what goes into a particular dish. Whether you are eating low carb or low fat, you can find (or construct) meals that fit your unique needs, and you do not need to worry about some of the problems attributed to other cooking methods. Slow cooking is typically a "moist" type of cooking, but unlike boiling, you end up eating all of the vitamin and mineral-rich broth. Unlike baking or frying, which necessitate relatively high temperatures (making those nasty polycyclic thingies), slow cooking occurs at reasonably low temperatures so that you don't see the wacky kitchen chemistry that is common with other approaches.

Economics

One of the most common refrains I hear about healthy eating is that "it's expensive." How folks find their health "expensive" is a head-scratcher to me, but let's just take this at face value and use the slow cooker as a tool to cut food costs. We do that by buying and cooking in bulk. That's it! Bulk buying tends to be less expensive, and when you cook in bulk, you save time and money in a variety of ways. One of the most important features I've found with this style of cooking is the ability to take relatively tough (but inexpensive) cuts of meat and make them taste great. Ribeye is obviously delicious, but unless you are a Google founder, it's not something you will eat daily due to cost considerations. With slow cooking, you can take an inexpensive rump roast and transform what might otherwise be best used to re-sole a shoe into a delicious, solid meal. We buy a lot of grass-fed meat, and while the fat content is low, the meat can be a bit tough. Standard cooking methods like grilling produce little more than an opportunity to exercise our chewing muscles! A slow cooker, a few hours, and some basic seasonings can transform the toughest grass-fed meat into a tasty meal.

Hopefully, I've sold you on the idea that slow cooking is a great idea, particularly for a Paleo lifestyle. So, what can you expect from this book? Essentially, the basics, done very well. By basics, I mean pretty standard American eats (with a few smart international contributions) that are quick and easy to make and will satisfy the most finicky palate. All bases are covered—breakfast, lunch, dinner, sides, and desserts. Although this is a cookbook, you will learn a little bit about my family (Chrissy is my sister-in-law, and her husband, Shawn, is my brother-in-law) and how neurotic Shawn is about his food. You'd think a former state wrestler and the Operations Manager for NorCal Strength & Conditioning would be pretty hearty when it comes to food, but Shawn is damn picky. This is not all bad, mind you! The benefits of this situation are three-fold: (1) I get to tease Shawn mercilessly at family functions, (2) Chrissy had to learn to be a very creative cook, and (3) If Shawn will eat these meals, you are guaranteed to love them.

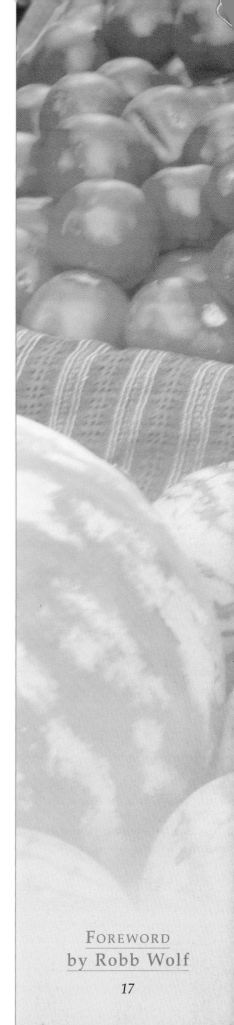

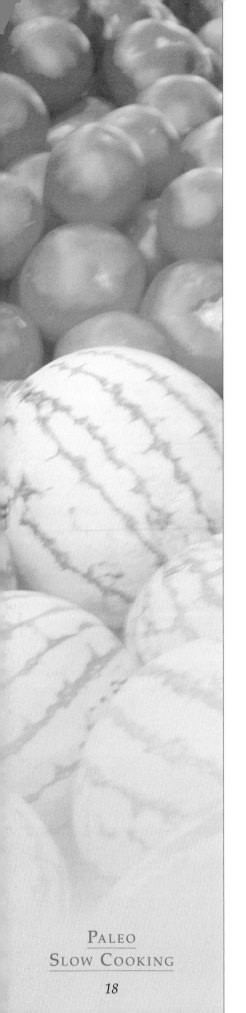

I came upon this Paleo concept almost fifteen years ago amidst terrible health issues. The decision to try Paleo at that time was easy for me since I had tried everything else. Lucky for me, the Paleo lifestyle literally saved my life. Since that time, I've helped hundreds of thousands of people "try" the Paleo way of eating, and it would appear that the results have been as profound for them as they've been for me. My greatest challenge has been, and continues to be, how to get folks to just "try" Paleo for 30 days, see how they look, feel, and perform, and critically evaluate if it is worth the effort. This book will make trying Paleo simpler. Preparing these meals is easy and fun, and it will leave you plenty of time to enjoy the energy and health that comes from this way of eating.

Viva
La Paleo!

Robb Wolf

Acknowledgments

First and foremost, to my husband Shawn, thank you for being my "realistic" voice throughout this project. Without your help, this book would have taken a lot longer to complete. Your countless trips to the grocery store, followed by your taste tests and your constructive, critical feedback, really helped to make this book happen. You are my best friend, a supportive husband, and an incredible father to our beautiful kids. I love you!

To my son, Kayden, you have changed my life in so many wonderful ways and so much so that it's hard to imagine my life without you. You are compassionate, fun, and seem to understand things far beyond your years. Your loving smile, sense of humor, and the sound of your laugh make my days complete. I love that even at three years old, you are protective of both your little sister and me. It shows me what an amazing person and big brother you are. With your imagination and willingness to try new things, you are my favorite helper in the kitchen. You were by my side helping me chop, season, and prep the majority of the recipes in this book, and I enjoyed every minute of it. I am so lucky to have you.

And Rylee, my beautiful baby girl, I cannot help but think you influenced the creation, flavors, and spices of many of these dishes. I look forward to sharing my love of cooking with you as you grow.

Glen Cordoza and Katie Deluca, the two of you are not only my friends and co-workers, but you were my neighbors throughout the majority of this book project. You were two of the first to taste my slow cooked creations, and the fact that you loved them every bit as much as I did encouraged me to move forward. Glen, you pushed me to take on the project during a crazy time in my life, and I want to thank you from the bottom of my heart for doing so. If it weren't for you, I probably would not have tackled it. Katie, I loved seeing your smiling face walk through the door at each of the photo shoots. I will never forget all of the sampling you did,

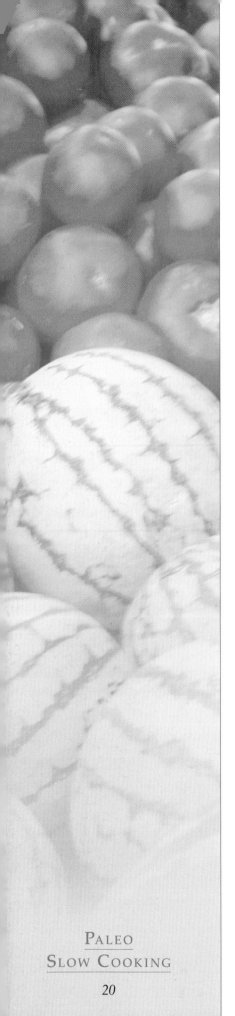

and if it weren't for you, I probably would have gained at least another twenty pounds during my pregnancy.

Robb Wolf and Nicki Violetti, the two of you play an incredible role in my life. Robb, if you had not met my sister, I am sure Nicki would still be a vegan, pestering me every time I eat a steak. Nicki, I am lucky to have a sister like you. You pushed me when we were kids to be a better athlete, and you push me now to become an even better person as an adult. You and I share a special bond that most will never understand. Thank you both for challenging me to eat better and for advising me to take on this project. Your help and support along the way has meant the world to me.

Sarah Fragoso, thank you for your invaluable insight and taste-testing along the way. Because of your experience with balancing family life and professional projects, you were one of the key role models for me during this project. I appreciate and respect your honesty and generosity in helping me. You are not just a friend—you are family. I will never forget our family dinners together after long photo shoots. I enjoyed anxiously awaiting the look of approval from your boys. John's typical feedback of "needs salt" will be an ongoing joke for years to come.

I owe a big thank you to Justin Scott for being my official taste-tester and for eating all of the extra food from the photo shoots. Your honest feedback and discerning palate have helped shape and season many of the dishes in this book, and I cannot thank you enough for that.

I owe a huge thank you to Dain Sandoval. Not only does Dain make me laugh and smile on a weekly basis, but he is also one of the most kind-hearted and generous individuals I know. Thank you for taking the time to be my farmer's market paparazzi.

To all of my co-workers in the NorCal Strength and Conditioning family—Katie, Glen, Jenny, Justin, Matt, and Jaime—thank you all for supporting me throughout this project. I am sure that a few of you may not even have been aware of the support you were giving, which to me is that much more special. Matt and Jaime, thank you for taking over my classes and clients while I was on maternity leave and finishing this book. Knowing that my personal training clients were in good hands and enjoying their sessions

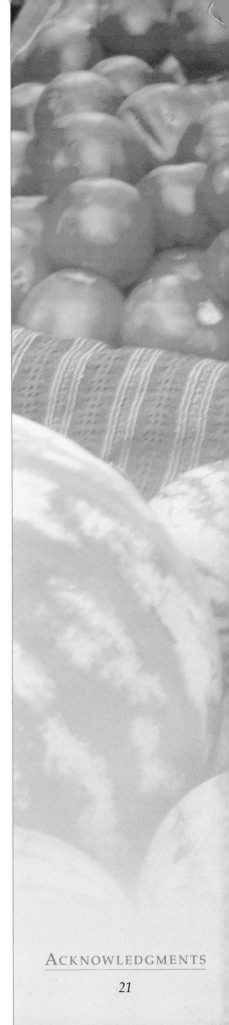

with you lifted a huge weight off of my shoulders. It's no secret that I'm passionate about what I do and enjoy working with each and every client at NorCal SC. The relationships that are built in our gym are unlike any other.

This brings me to the rest of my NorCal SC family—the clients. All of our clients remind me every day why I love my job. Thank you all for giving me a huge extended family that is completely irreplaceable.

To my beautiful cousin, Nina, at Nina Turek Photography, thank you so much for offering to photograph my family. We couldn't be more pleased with the photos you took and are so happy that we were able to include them in this book.

Thank you, Ammin Nut Company and the Stuber family, for supplying me with your phenomenal products throughout this project. Your Ammin butters are, by far, the best I have ever tasted, and your Ammin flours are simply amazing.

Shannon Rosan, this book would not be the same without you! It's not easy making food in a slow cooker that looks as good as it tastes. Your attention to detail and creative style is beautifully showcased in each dish. Thank you for making my dishes look amazing!

To my publisher, Erich Krauss, I appreciate your giving me the opportunity to share my recipes with a wider audience. Thank you for your continued effort to make this book exactly what I wanted it to be. I know it wasn't easy working with a pregnant woman. Thank you for being realistic, understanding, and making this a smooth process.

I owe a huge thank you to Kelly Milton for being my personal prop shopper while I was pregnant and for being such an essential part of my creative design team. Thank you for being a great friend and volunteering so much of your time to bring this project to completion.

Julie and Charles Mayfield, thank you for being the beautiful people you are. I appreciate your opinions and the feedback that you both offered me throughout this project … and the video clips of Buzz, too!

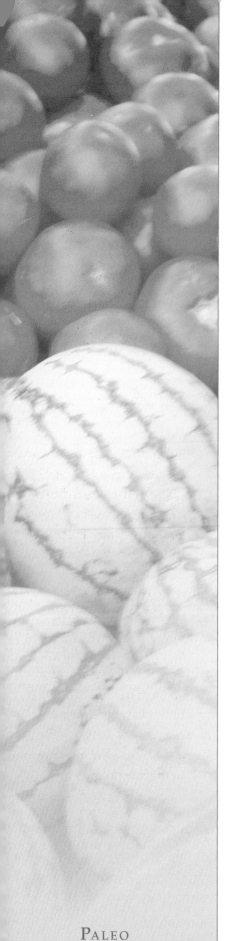

Laura Damschen and Terri Akers, your friendship is beyond that of the client/trainer relationship. It is one that I will forever treasure. Laura, thank you for being a great thinker and creative cook, offering me problem-solving strategies in the kitchen. Terri, thank you for being so caring and making me laugh. Although I was exhausted, I will never forget when you both came to visit me in the hospital after having Rylee. The fact that you asked me how the book was coming along meant more to me than you will ever know.

Thank you to my husband's family. Robin, my sweet and fun sister-in-law, thank you for sharing some of your favorite family recipes. Thank you, Gayle, Shane, and Jessi for watching Kayden and being so understanding and flexible. Knowing that Kayden was having a blast with you guys made my life a little easier.

Aunt Linda, your timely Facebook and email messages filled with your positive energy meant so much during this project, and they helped me to motor through. Thank you!

Dad, where would I be without you? I could not ask for a better father or grandfather for my kids. Thank you for always listening and offering comforting words of guidance and encouragement.

Penny, thank you for being so great with Kayden and always so willing to get in a water fight! I love watching you both run and play with Kayden. The sound of his laughter and the look on his face is always priceless.

Mom, not a day goes by when I don't think of you or am reminded of you. Your spirit has been with me every step of the way. I see you in myself and in my children. You always said that I could do anything if I put my mind to it, and completing this book during my pregnancy with Rylee proved that to be true. Mom, you have helped shape me and make my life better than I could have possibly imagined. Thank you for showing me that anything is possible with a positive attitude and that "life is truly what you make it." For that, I am forever grateful!

Introduction

My goal in writing this book is to provide a guide that anyone can use to prepare healthy Paleo meals with a slow cooker. Slow cooking is one of the easiest, oldest, and most forgiving methods of cooking. You don't need to have a culinary green thumb. The busy mom, the time-crunched/penny pinching graduate student, and the kitchen-phobic bachelor can all make wonderful meals with a slow cooker.

There are many excuses that arise when people are considering a dietary or lifestyle change. Time and expense are two that top the list. Our modern lifestyles do not often lend themselves to hours in the kitchen. Work schedules, parenting duties, and other miscellaneous responsibilities make it easy for us to dismiss the importance of home cooked meals and opt instead for fast food. After a long, stressful day, the majority of us aren't pining to spend another hour or two in the kitchen preparing dinner.

This is where the slow cooker becomes a life saver!

Slow cooking is all about easy! Simply gather and prepare your ingredients, and *all* ingredients go into one pot. They can be left for hours to safely cook while you are away at work or play. And the best part: you have just *one* pot to clean!

The recipes in this book take little time, and many can be prepared well ahead of your scheduled meal. As a bonus, the typical cuts of meat used in slow cooker recipes are among the most affordable, making slow cooking a viable option for everyone.

I've divided the book into five sections: Breakfast, Soups and Stews, Main Dishes, Side Dishes, and Desserts. The Main Dishes and Soups and Stews sections are full of hearty and meaty dishes, many of which are old family recipes that I have converted to suit my family's Paleo lifestyle. The Sides section contains several dishes that can be prepared in minutes to accompany the main dishes that have been cooking in your slow cooker all day.

Prep the night before!

If you don't have time in the morning to gather and prep your ingredients for your slow cooker meal, you can do it the night before. Wash and chop vegetables, add meat and spices, and put it in the slow cooker stoneware and place in the refrigerator overnight. When you wake up, place the stoneware in the slow cooker base, and turn it on. You can do this while waiting for your morning coffee to brew!

Tips for slow cooking success:

- *Invest in a deep freeze*
- *Keep cuts of meat on hand in the freezer*
- *Keep your spice cupboard well stocked*
- *Save money on beef by buying a quarter or half of a grass-fed cow*

Don't lift the lid!

Every time you lift the lid of your slow cooker, steam escapes, and you will need to increase the cooking time by twenty minutes.

I have also included a few tasty breakfast recipes that can be easily modified based on the ingredients you have on hand. And ... drumroll, please—you'll also find a dessert section with five easy Paleo desserts.

Breakfast and Dessert in a slow cooker?

To be honest, I didn't consider cooking breakfast or dessert in my slow cooker for a long time because it seemed such meals would be easier to prepare on the stove or in the oven. This is often true, but there are certain occasions like potlucks, brunches, or even the holidays when your oven or stove space is limited. When this happens, a few slow cooker recipes will come in handy.

As for the desserts, I have become partial to using the slow cooker, as I find that desserts come out moister than when prepared in a conventional oven. All of the breakfast and dessert recipes in this book can also be prepared on the stove or in the oven to best fit your preferences and time constraints.

Your recipe modifications

You'll find a small blank "recipe card" at the bottom of each recipe. This is for any notes you may have after making each dish. For example you may prefer your food extra spicy and might make a note on the chili verde recipe to add an extra jalapeño. With your notes on the recipe page you will easily be able to see any changes you want to experiment with the next time you make it.

I hope you enjoy your foray into Paleo slow cooking! Regardless of your budget, schedule, or aptitude in the kitchen, you can use these recipes to feed yourself and your family well.

Enjoy!

Before...

After...

My Story:

How I came to be the author of a Paleo slow cooking book

I am continually amazed by how events shape the course of our lives. There are many things that happen to us that have far more significance than we grasp in the moment. Only in hindsight do we realize the ripple effects.

In 2003, my graduating year at California State University of Chico, my mother passed away. She was fifty years young. I was twenty-three. She had suffered from Rheumatoid Arthritis since her early twenties and had been managing it with medications and surgery. She had her first hip replacement surgery when I was seven years old, but it was a foot surgery in November of 2002 that created a cascade of medical mishaps that ultimately led to her death nine months later.

Losing a parent at any age is horrible, but when you are young and your parent is not "old," it's even worse. Watching my mother pass away left me feeling utterly helpless and alone. That was undoubtedly the toughest year of my life.

After her death, I lost sight of who I was, as well as the importance of my own health. I paid no attention to the foods I ate, and I drank a fair amount of alcohol. I went from a really active and healthy college girl to a lost, heartbroken, college graduate. I have no idea what I weighed during this time of my life. I just know I felt unhealthy and uncomfortable in my own skin.

Losing our mom brought my sister, Nicki, and I much closer together. She had moved to Chico in January of 2003 to be closer to home and closer to mom, who was in and out of the hospital at that time. Nicki and I had always had a good relationship, but we were never really close. So, I treasured our new relationship. But this is also why I hated Robb Wolf the first time I met him.

I was eating my standard breakfast: a bacon, egg, and cheese bagel sandwich at a local coffee shop where my sister was working at the time. Robb and Nicki had just started dating, and he frequently stopped in while she worked. He pulled up a chair and interrupted my bagel sandwich and double mocha. I remember feeling extremely annoyed and entirely unimpressed by the geeky guy who was stealing my sister's time.

We now laugh when we think back at how incredibly mean I was to him. I had never heard of "gluten free," and his quirky dietary habits did not improve my impression of him. I didn't fully understand the severity of his gluten sensitivity, and I don't think I cared all that much. Nicki tells me that when Robb joined us on Thanksgiving for the first time, I knowingly tried to contaminate him with crouton crumbs. I don't remember being that mean.

Shortly after Robb opened his gym in Chico, Nicki, my dad, and I all started training with him. It felt great to exercise again, and it was wonderful for the three of us to train together. It was healing both physically and emotionally. I began to feel better, stronger, and more fit than I had in quite a while. Then, Robb challenged me to eat real food.

Up until this point I was dragging my feet on making any changes to my diet. I loved the workouts and training with my family, but was reluctant to change what I ate. I made a few small changes, but was not fully on board.

Then I met Shawn; I fell in love and completely fell off the wagon... for three years! Our new relationship made it way too easy to slip out of my routine and into a new one with him. Shawn was raised on Top Ramen, Hamburger Helper, and grilled cheese sandwiches and, as an adult, hadn't really deviated from this fare. I went from prioritizing my health and fitness and working out three to four times a week, to avoiding the gym entirely. We consistently

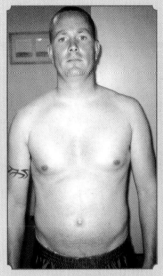

Before...

After...

Paleo pregnancy tips:

· *Leftovers: When you're pregnant, leftovers are key! Make enough food so that you have plenty for storing. The slow cooker is great for this.*

· *Snacks: Have healthy snacks on hand like beef jerky, hard-boiled eggs, nuts, seeds, veggie sticks, and fresh seasonal fruit.*

· *Graze: Eat several smaller meals throughout the day as opposed to three or four large meals.*

skipped breakfast, ate almost all of our meals out, and drank our daily share of soda and blended mochas. Our busy schedule only fed our unhealthy habits. Between working full time and going to school for my Masters in Education and teaching credential, I was convinced I had no time to cook real food.

It was the death of Shawn's father in May of 2007 that prompted us to reevaluate our lifestyle and commit to changing for good. After watching his father take his last breath, Shawn told me, "I don't want to die like that." It's sad that it sometimes takes a serious illness or death to cause us to face our own mortality and become motivated enough to make a change in our own lives.

We came to the realization that we needed to change, and we were finally ready. The very next day, my husband and I started to implement all of the things that Robb had taught me a few years before. I knew what we needed to do, but now we actually needed to do it. We needed to make time for ourselves and make "us" (individually speaking) a priority. We stocked the pantry, stopped eating out, and relearned our way around the kitchen. We also quit drinking soda and mochas and made time to get back to the gym for regular exercise.

Our first three months back in the gym, we took personal training sessions with Robb. Not only did he kick our butts, but he also helped us understand the importance of food quality and gut health. In just a few short months, we felt great and looked so much better.

Shawn and I established a healthy routine and lifestyle just as our life and work started to get crazy again. It's easy to justify and rationalize any excuse for not making a change or for jumping off the wagon the first chance you get. But this time it was different. Having a partner in the process really helped. We could share the struggles, the cravings, and the withdrawals, and this helped us keep each other on track.

We were determined to maintain the healthier lifestyle we had established together, especially when we received news in March of 2008 that we were expecting our first child in October. It was clear that it was more important than ever to make this dietary change our permanent lifestyle.

Here I was pregnant, working full-time, and finishing up my Masters degree in Education. I was tired, but we continued making time for the gym and preparing meals ahead of time. I found that it was even more important during the pregnancy to be prepared with meals and snacks around the clock.

Why Slow Cooking?

My husband, Shawn, is pickier about food than any adult I've ever known. For example, when we first started dating eight years ago, the only source of "real" protein he would consume was a boneless, skinless chicken breast. It had to be fully trimmed of any fat, veins, or anything else that looked "funny" to him. The switch to eating real food or Paleo was not as easy for Shawn as it was for me, and his pickiness limited the variety I attempted in the kitchen. It definitely made my job as the primary cook in our household more difficult.

Prior to my slow cooking adventure, we had a fairly repetitive menu. Like most people, I had four or five "go-to" meals that I

In 2008, I gave birth to our son, Kayden. He was healthy, and Shawn and I were elated. Kayden has changed our lives in so many wonderful ways. He showed us, and continues to show us, what is important in life. Living a healthy lifestyle for us is not about having the fastest gym records or the latest and greatest new toy. For us, it is about being able to play with our kids and watch them grow up. Staying healthy and fit and being good role models are our priorities—so much so that these priorities prompted a career change for us both.

I started working at NorCal Strength and Conditioning in 2009. I found that working with clients in the gym gave me the same emotional reward that I received from teaching. I love knowing that what I'm doing is making a difference. I see a little bit of myself in each of my clients, and watching the changes they make week after week is incredibly rewarding. My parents had urged me to find a job or career that I loved, and I have found just that at NorCal Strength and Conditioning.

repeated week after week. My busy schedule didn't allow me to spend too much time or energy branching out from our standard fare, and I wasn't overly ambitious in this regard since previous experimentation attempts had been rejected.

So, what changed? In October of 2011, we found out that we were expecting our second child. Suddenly, it was even more important to have our meals planned ahead. I was completely exhausted after work, and the reality of needing to prepare food after coming home, while also wanting to play with my three-year-old, was more than I could handle. I remembered that my mother used a slow cooker now and then when I was a kid, so I pulled mine out of the cabinet and began to experiment. I tried some of my old family recipes, tweaking them to make them suitable for my family's Paleo lifestyle.

I was so pleased with the way they turned out! The food was tender, tasty, and, better yet, my family loved it! Low and behold, I had found my savior. I could spend a few minutes in the morning loading my slow cooker or even give Shawn some simple instructions and ingredients, and I could then come home to a nice, warm, home-cooked meal. What more could I ask for?

With such great reviews from my picky husband (who was not only eating these meals but the leftovers, too), I started sharing some of the recipes with our friends, neighbors, clients, and co-workers. I was so excited to discover that my slow cooked creations were a hit that I started experimenting with a few breakfast and dessert ideas. I was amazed at the versatility of this often-overlooked kitchen appliance! Before I knew it, I had a wide array of meals and recipes that my whole family could enjoy. I'm happy to have the opportunity to share these with you.

Slow Cooking:
It's Truly Paleo!

There is evidence that people have been cooking "slow" for a few hundred thousand years. Numerous cultures from around the world have used pit cooking and earth ovens to slowly cook meats, tubers, and starches. Pit cooking involved a pit lined with hot, fire-heated stones that were filled with meat and vegetation and covered with dirt to seal in the heat and cook with steam. More recently, traditional American barbeque was cooked in a hole in the ground, although it's uncommon to find it prepared this way today. (For more about the history of pit cooking, visit this website: http://www.foodbuzz.com/recipes/3062883-pit-cooking-some-history.)

Now, fortunately, we don't have to dig a hole and build a fire in our backyard to enjoy the flavors that come from foods that have been slow cooked. Thanks to the invention of the slow cooker about sixty years ago, you can do it from one pot on your kitchen counter. With this book as your guide, your kitchen time will be simplified, and enjoying home cooked meals will become a reality.

Selecting Your Slow Cooker

Slow cookers come in a variety of sizes with several different features. Popular brands include Hamilton Beach, Rival, Sunbeam, and Crock-Pot®. Most new slow cooker models have removable stoneware, some of which can even be used in the oven and on the stovetop. Be sure to read your instruction manual before using yours in this way. Other great slow cooker features include digital thermometers, programmable timers, and auto shut-off.

All recipes in this book have been prepared and tested in a six-quart slow cooker, which is perfect for a family of four or will leave you ample leftovers for a smaller family. If you are cooking just for yourself, you can get away with a smaller unit (one or two quarts), although a larger size will allow you to have more leftovers.

My personal favorite is the six-quart Hamilton Beach Set 'n Forget programmable slow cooker. This cooker features removable stoneware and high, medium, and low settings. The removable stoneware makes cleaning much easier than the older models. I remember needing to be extra careful to avoid getting the cord wet when I was a kid trying to clean my mother's old slow cooker. The Hamilton Beach Set 'n Forget model has another great feature: It automatically switches to warm after the cooking time is complete so that your food stays warm until you are ready to eat it. Additionally, it has a probe thermometer that you can use for large cuts of meat to ensure that they're cooked thoroughly. While these features are certainly nice, you will be able to make wonderful, healthy, home-cooked Paleo meals regardless of the size, make, or model of your slow cooker.

My favorite slow cooker features:

· *Programmable cook time*

· *Automatic switch to warm*

· *Latching lid*

Keep your stoneware safe!

Be sure to let your slow cooker cool completely before washing the stoneware. Using cold water on your hot stoneware could cause it to crack.

Raising a Paleo Family

Raising a Paleo family has some challenges, but no more than any other family. Like all parents, we are raising our children in the way we believe is the best. We're committed to preparing the majority of our family's meals at home with ingredients that we choose. I know that I won't always be able to control what my children eat, but I can control the foods I have in the house and the meals I prepare. I like knowing what goes into each dish. We frequently talk about the food we eat and where it comes from. I try to take advantage of all teachable moments in the kitchen, the grocery store, or at the farmers market. It's quality time we can spend together and valuable as the kids learn about food and how to cook.

Perhaps the greatest challenges come when your kids are in school around grain-based, sugar-laden foods that the other kids are eating. Teaching your children about the foods they eat is one way to minimize much of this exposure. Kayden understands that gluten can hurt his belly, and he knows the reasons we don't drink milk. When he was younger and asked me for something that was grain-based, I simply explained that we don't eat food containing gluten. Now that he is in preschool, he notices that other kids drink milk and that they have different snacks, but he doesn't seem to give it a second thought. He always asks the teacher if what they are going to eat contains gluten, and I feel blessed that the teachers at his preschool are very accommodating.

My husband and I feel strongly about making dinnertime a family-centered time. I come from a family that ate dinner together every night unless we had a basketball game or other afterschool event. We don't bring our phones to the dinner table, the TV is off, and it's a time to talk and share the events of our day.

But there are certainly situations that are inherently more challenging. In such cases, I find that a bit of flexibility and creativity can help. As an example, we took Kayden to Disneyland in De-

Little helpers in the kitchen

Get your kids involved in the kitchen by having them help. Little hands can easily be guided to assist with the following:

· *Stirring*

· *Measuring*

· *Cutting, chopping (find a kid-safe knife!)*

· *Adding spices*

· *Setting the slow cooker, on/off, etc.*

· *Tasting the ingredients*

* Kids like to taste the foods they help prepare, so this is a great way to get them to try new things.

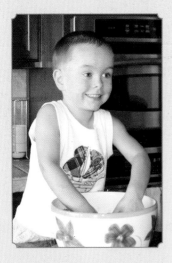

cember 2011, and as you can imagine, the food options were far from optimal. We made the best of the situation by ordering our hamburgers without the bun and went on with our day. I think it's essential to let your kids be a part of the process when it comes to food, whether you're preparing it yourself or in one of those suboptimal situations like at a theme park.

Perhaps I run the risk of my kids hating me when they get older for never giving them Lucky Charms for breakfast or allowing them to drink soda. Only time will tell. I feel good about the lifestyle and food decisions we have chosen. We believe in the importance of a good foundation for our kids.

If you are transitioning your family from a more standard American diet, it may be difficult at first. But over time, as you talk about food quality and incorporate healthier eating habits in the house, you will start to see your family develop healthier eating habits outside of the house as well.

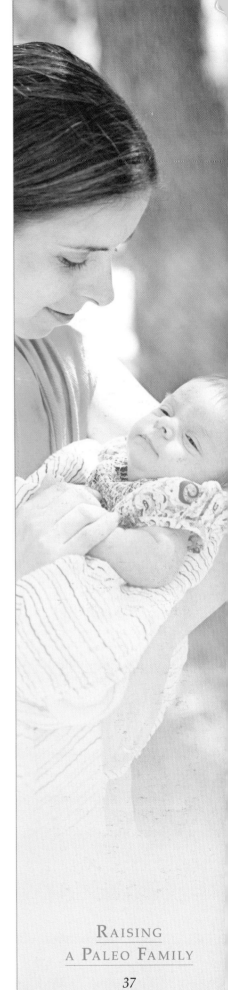

Health benefits of eating Paleo

- *Decrease inflammation*
- *Improve blood lipids*
- *Decrease body fat*
- *Increase mental clarity*
- *Potentially reverse autoimmune disease*
- *Forestall the aging process*
- *Prevent neurodegenerative disease*
- *Improve athletic performance*

The Benefits of Eating Paleo

I have been following a Paleo lifestyle since mid 2007 and have been coaching my clients at the gym in Paleo since early 2009. I can easily explain the basics, especially when it comes to implementation.

The personal benefits are obvious. Eating this way not only helps me feel better and look better, it also enables me to have the energy necessary to keep up with my extremely active family. I want to have the energy to run and play with my kids, and I want to be able to watch them grow up, get married, and have their own kids (if that is where their journey takes them). I want to simply be there for them. Kids should not have to watch their parents die at a young age, yet this happens all too often. I can't help but wonder if the outcome would have been different for my mom if she had learned this way of eating. In hindsight, however, I may not be where I am today.

If you want to learn more about the science behind Paleo, I highly recommend that you read and reread Robb Wolf's *The Paleo Solution*.

In my case, eating this way just made sense, and a "challenge" was presented to me at just the right time. Thank you, Robb, for introducing my family and me to this wonderful lifestyle.

Slow Cooker Food Matrix

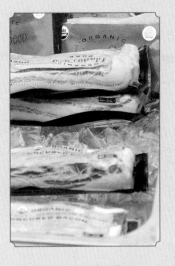

Robb created the original Food Matrix as a way to share how easy it can be to combat boredom when cooking Paleo meals. By making a list of proteins, vegetables, fats, and herbs and spices, you can choose one item (or a combination of items) from each column and construct an almost infinite number of meals!

With a couple of slight tweaks, the Food Matrix lends itself perfectly to slow cooking. Because we tend to use fattier cuts of meat in the slow cooker, unless you're making a curry, there is really no reason to add fat to your slow cooked meals. A couple of my recipes contain either olive oil or coconut milk, but most rely on the fat naturally occurring in the meats.

NOTE:

You'll find that I've left out fish and seafood from my list of best slow cooked meats. You can cook fish and seafood in a slow cooker, but it needs to be added toward the end of the cooking cycle. My aim in this book is to only include recipes that you can set and leave, so aside from a shrimp recipe, I've chosen to omit seafood.

Best Slow Cooked Meats:

Beef:

Rump roast

Shoulder

Chuck

Shanks

Rounds

Short ribs

Stew meat

Brisket

Rib roast

Pork:

Shoulder

Ham

Roast

Ribs

Chops

Lamb:

Shoulder

Shanks

Leg

Poultry:

Chicken breasts

Chicken thighs

Chicken legs

Ground turkey

Turkey breasts

Turkey legs

Best Slow Cooked Vegetables:

<u>*Onions*</u>

<u>*Carrots*</u>

<u>*Celery*</u>

<u>*Butternut squash*</u>

<u>*Zucchini**</u>

<u>*Pumpkin*</u>

<u>*Bell peppers*</u>

<u>*Mushrooms**</u>

<u>*Sweet potatoes*</u>

<u>*Yams*</u>

<u>*Cabbage*</u>

<u>*Spinach*</u>

<u>*Kale*</u>

<u>*Peppers*</u>

*Some people prefer adding these vegetables toward the end of the cooking cycle to retain more of their original texture

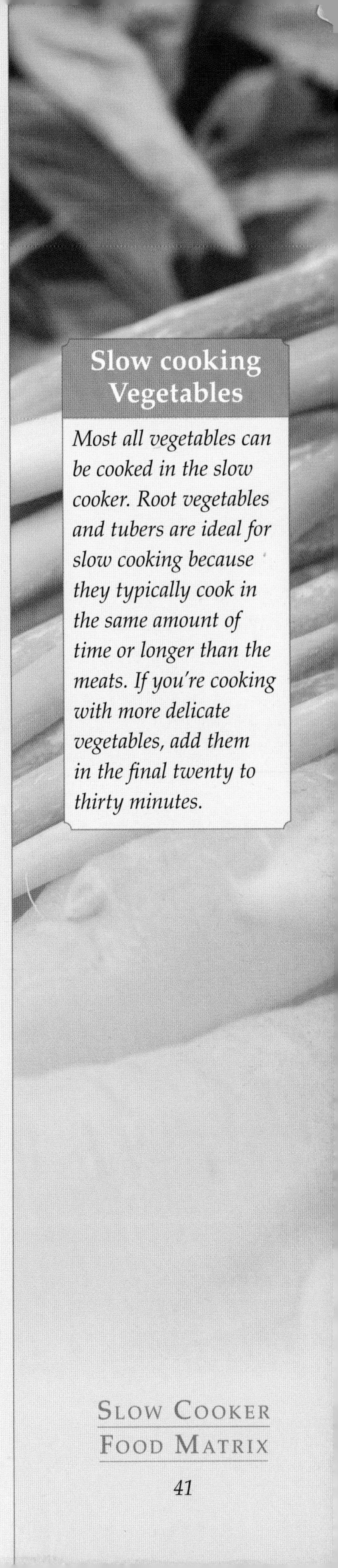

Slow cooking Vegetables

Most all vegetables can be cooked in the slow cooker. Root vegetables and tubers are ideal for slow cooking because they typically cook in the same amount of time or longer than the meats. If you're cooking with more delicate vegetables, add them in the final twenty to thirty minutes.

Spices for Slow Cooking:

Garlic	*Paprika*
Curry	*Cardamom*
Ginger	*Cinnamon*
Pepper	*Salt*
Oregano	*Black pepper*
Cumin	*Rosemary*
Chipotle powder	*Cilantro*
Chili powder	*Coriander*
Basil	

A note on using spices in your slow cooker:

When cooking in your slow cooker, you can use both fresh and dried herbs. If you are using fresh herbs, preserve their flavors by adding them at the end of the cooking cycle. Add dried herbs at the beginning, and then, adjust the herbs and spices at the end of the cooking cycle to taste. This is the way my mother did it, and it works well. As you will see in my recipes, I typically prefer using dried herbs, simply for convenience. I like to put all of my ingredients in at the beginning, but you can adjust the seasonings in any of my recipes to fit your family's palate. If you prefer a milder flavor or have a particularly delicate palate, I suggest adding half of the herbs and spices at the beginning of the cooking process and the remainder at the end so that you can make adjustments.

Fats:

Coconut milk

Coconut oil

Olive oil

Rarely is it necessary to add fat to a slow cooked meal. Typically, the fat already inherent in the meat is adequate to produce savory meals. Still, some people prefer to remove the skin from chicken thighs and legs or the excess fat from beef. The skin on the chicken will not brown and can easily be removed prior to or even after the cooking process (remember my picky husband who removes the skin prior to eating chicken). I rarely trim beef unless there is an excessive layer of fat (again to accommodate my husband) or if a recipe recommends the fat to be trimmed.

Ammin Nut Company

I am fortunate to live in Chico, California "where the nuts come from!" As our city's tagline suggests, we are surrounded by orchards. One of my favorite nut companies, and the one whose products I use exclusively in this book, is Ammin Nut Company. Their almond butter and almond flour are superior to any I have found at supermarkets. You can order their products online at www.amminnut.com. Of course, local is best, so if you have access to local nut products in your area, use those. (Almonds are actually pronounced "ammins" by the folks who grow them. If you come to Chico and ask for "almonds," be sure to pronounce it "ammins" in order to fit right in with the locals.)

Cooking Utensils

Bowls

small mixing
bowl

medium mixing
bowl

large mixing
bowl

Knifes

paring
knife

serrated
knife

chefs knife

Measuring tools

measuring
cups

measuring
spoons

Storage

airtight
containers

Specialty

zester

lime
squeezer

garlic press

julienne
slicer

 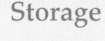

Remove food from stoneware prior to refrigerating/ storing!

It's best to store your food in an airtight container, not in the stoneware. Also, the stoneware takes up far too much real estate in the fridge!

Power Tools

| _food processor_ | _blender_ | _slow cooker_ | _hand mixer_ | **BBQ** |

Pots / Pans / Skillets

| _skillet_ | _sauté pan_ | _large soup pot_ | _roasting pan_ | _square baking dish_ | _baking sheet_ |

Kitchen Accessories

| _spatula_ | _tongs_ | _can opener_ | _peeler_ | _whisk_ | _potato masher_ | _kitchen shears_ |

| _cutting board_ | _salad spinner_ | _ladle_ | _spoon_ | _large slotted spoon_ |

Cooking Tactics

Knife Skills

How do you know whether to chop something, mince it, or dice it? Much of this depends on the desired feel and texture, how you want the flavors to penetrate the dish, and the final presentation you want.

Aesthetics and Presentation

How you prepare a particular item will dramatically change the final presentation. Julienne (long thin strips) will, of course, make a very different visual impression than puréeing, which turns the item into a paste.

Cooking Qualities

The more you process a food, the faster it will cook. You will also get more flavor faster from vigorous processing as you increase the surface area of the item.

Slow Cooking Takes the Pressure Off Your Processing Choice

Compared to other cooking methods, slow cooking is pretty forgiving in terms of the type of knife-wielding skills you use. Due to the fact that slow cooking makes things very tender, even to the point of falling apart if cooked long enough, it's often unnecessary to be particular about the way you process your ingredients. You might want to be a little more particular when preparing an item for a garnish (green onions to garnish a Mexican-style soup, for example). Be creative and play with each of the following techniques, but keep in mind that the various preparation methods are mainly important for the aesthetics of garnishes and not critical for one-pot slow cooking.

Chopping

Chopping is the "shooting from the hip" knife skill. Take a whole onion, carrot, or bell pepper, and simply reduce it to smaller pieces. You do not need to be overly concerned with the size of the pieces. Cut to size based on your preference. Keep in mind that the larger the pieces, the longer they typically take to cook.

How to chop:

How you chop is somewhat determined by what you are chopping. A carrot might simply be cut into discs. Then, you work the carrots into a pile and "chop" the knife through the discs making smaller, irregularly shaped pieces. Easy! You can also cut the carrot in half lengthwise and into quarters so that you have carrot pieces that are round on one side and flat on the other. Then, you "chop" these pieces crosswise to make smaller pieces.

For an onion, cut off the top and bottom, peel it, and cut it in half from top to bottom. Then, cut that piece into quarters from top to bottom. You are effectively making wedges at this stage, which are then cross-cut, finishing your "chop."

Why chop?

Chopping is easy! You do not need to be overly concerned about sizes or uniformity of the pieces.

Keep root vegetables small!

If you are careful to cut root vegetables like sweet potatoes and carrots into small, uniform pieces (like one-inch cubes), they will cook evenly and at about the same rate as the meat. Larger pieces take much longer to cook thoroughly.

Cooking
Tactics

Slicing

Slicing is a great technique for presentation. You can slice items into thin discs, cutting across the length of the item, much like you would slice a lemon or cucumber to add to ice water. You can also slice an item like a tomato into quarters by cutting it in half from top to bottom twice. It offers a completely different look, but both methods are still slicing.

How to slice:

As mentioned above, you can slice in a variety of ways. An item like a tomato can be sliced into quarters or discs.

Why slice?

Slicing is fast, easy, and can dramatically alter the presentation of your dish, depending upon the exact way you slice.

Dicing

Dicing is one of the most common of food preparation methods. When you dice, you aim for uniform size and shape (cubes). Normally, you cut into somewhat long, rectangular pieces. Then, you cross-cut.

How to dice:

As with all cutting techniques, how you dice will be somewhat dependent on what item you are dicing. For a carrot, follow the beginning procedure for carrots, but be careful to produce uniform sizes and shapes when making the final cross-cuts.

Why dice?

Dicing is great for garnishes and when you want small, uniform pieces of vegetables like onions, carrots, and bell peppers.

Shredding

Shredding is a method of producing thin, reasonably uniform pieces. Think about the consistency of cabbage used in cole slaw or sauerkraut. Shredding can be used for anything from chicken to cabbage to onions, but it works best with items that have either layers or a very well defined "grain" (like the muscle fiber direction in chicken).

How to shred:

For cabbage or onions, cut in half from top to bottom. Then, slice off very thin sections, cutting across the layers.

Why shred?

Shredding is great way to get veggies ready for condiments or to get chicken, beef, or pork ready for a lettuce wrap. Meats become so tender in the slow cooker that you can often shred them just using two forks. For vegetables, it's especially nice if you have a food processor, but even with a knife, it's fast and easy!

Mincing

Mincing is just a step down from turning an item into a paste. A piece of ginger root, for example, is pretty tough and fibrous, yet has lots of flavor. Mincing is how you best release that flavor.

How to mince:

First, slice the item into very thin strips or discs. Turn it crosswise and continue slicing thinly. Continue this process until the pieces are very small. Again, think about trying to make a paste using a knife. You will never really get to a paste consistency, but depending on your needs for a particular dish, you'll want to come close.

Why mince?

Mincing is typically used with spices like garlic and ginger. It involves cutting the item into the smallest possible sizes without puréeing. Mincing allows the flavors of the small pieces to thoroughly integrate into your recipe.

Puréeing

Since purée is French in derivation, it is instantly sexy and sophisticated. In reality, it's simply turning a food into a paste. Think mashed potatoes, creamy soups, and sauces.

How to purée:

An item is typically cooked first, then passed through a food processor or blender. Not much technique here. This is a great way to make old standards like sweet potatoes (which turn out fantastically in the slow cooker) and jazz them up.

Why purée?

Puréeing is a great method to make a food more easily digestible or as an easy way to create a creamy, "mashed potatoes" type of consistency.

Why cook at all?

by Robb Wolf

I'm assuming you have already bought this book or are simply thumbing through it madly in the bookstore. If you are at home reading through this, you might ask the question, "Why cook at all? And if I do cook, are there any specific health benefits to slow cooking?"

The potential of not cooking anything, just eating our food raw, would solve a host of problems, right? No pots and pans! Think of the time you'd save! Well, while there are some folks in the world who are pretty adamant that eating raw food is always the way to go, the science simply does not back this up. In his book, *Catching Fire: How Cooking Made us Human*, Professor of Biological Anthropology at Harvard University, Richard Wrangham makes a pretty tight case that cooking was a major driver in human evolution. About two million years ago, the human lineage made some dramatic changes. Our ancestors' gastrointestinal tracts shrank while our brains grew. This is called the "expensive tissue hypothesis," and it helps to explain how eating a nutrient-rich, largely cooked diet helped us to become who we are. Our shrinking digestive systems and growing brains were a biological trade-off that was driven by changes in our food and how we consumed that food (cooked). The results have been pretty impressive!

If you are not a fan of that whole wacky "evolutionary theory," science still makes a strong argument for why cooking in general is a good thing, and slow cooking in particular is a great thing. Not surprisingly, it relates back to digestibility, so let's look at the macronutrients protein, carbohydrate, and fat to see how cooking actually improves nutrient absorption.

Protein

Most folks in Paleo land can identify good protein sources (chicken, fish, other meat) from poor protein sources (beans+rice, corn+squash, or what we call "third world proteins," because they will keep you alive but will not make you thrive). Few people know that proteins can have up to four different structural considerations, however.

Primary Structure

The primary structure of a protein is the sequence of amino acids that comprise the protein. In normal terrestrial biology, we usually encounter twenty-one amino acids, and this is what everything from steaks to feathers to silk are made from. Imagine each of these twenty-one amino acids being somewhat like a child's building block, each different from the others. The primary structure is only concerned with which amino acids are strung together in what pattern. This pattern can be visualized simply as a long chain.

Secondary Structure

Secondary protein structure is a result of the shapes of the individual amino acids and how they fit together next to one another. In biology, many of these structures end up looking a lot like a spiral staircase.

Tertiary Structure

Tertiary structure can best be visualized by taking a spiral staircase and wrapping it around itself, making a variety of shapes ranging from spheres to tubes.

Quaternary Structure

Take one protein chain in which its tertiary structure is a sphere, and another in which the tertiary structure is a tube. Now, put them together. That combination is what organic chemists call the quaternary structure of protein. Essentially, this structure consists of two (or more) separate protein entities that are stuck together.

What the heck does any of this have to do with cooking and digestion? Well, we only absorb proteins in the form of single or, at most, two amino acid pieces. So, when we consume protein, we need to break down all of the aforementioned structures, leaving only amino acids to pass through the small intestine. Cooking can break down most of the quaternary structures and some of the tertiary structures. Our digestive enzymes are pretty good at breaking down the secondary and primary structures of protein, but not so great at whole, intact protein with the tertiary and quaternary structures intact. There are non-heat cooking methods such as acid cooking (lemon or lime juice) or brining (high salt content) which also help to destabilize the protein and make it more amenable to our digestive enzymes. Low-heat cooking helps to break down proteins very effectively and does so without creating some problematic chemical products like polycyclic aromatic hydrocarbons (common in high-heat grilling and also carcinogenic). From a digestibility and palatability standpoint, slow cooking is a winner-winner chicken dinner!

Carbohydrate

It may come as a surprise, but if you eat something like a sweet potato raw, it does not digest very well. In fact, it really does not digest much at all. We do pretty well with things like fruit, which are primarily composed of simple sugars, but our digestion is designed such that starch must be cooked to make it digestible. Starch is a long string of glucose molecules that can be folded in various shapes, somewhat similar to the tertiary structure of proteins. Constant heat gelatinizes starch granules, thus making them amenable to the action of our salivary and pancreatic amylases.

Fat

Fat digestibility is not significantly altered during cooking, but high temperature cooking can damage (oxidize) fragile polyunsaturated fats. Slow cooking wins again, as the cooking temperature is much lower than grilling, for example, while the slow cooker design limits airflow, thus minimizing oxidation.

Micronutrient Absorption

Most people are aware that if you boil broccoli, you are likely better off drinking the water the broccoli was boiled in than eating the wilted greens, as the bulk of the vitamins, minerals, and antioxidants have found their way into the water. Most people are not aware, however, that cooking dramatically increases the absorption of a host of nutrients such as beta-carotene, a vitamin A precursor and potent antioxidant. Slow cooking offers the best middle road, as we keep all of the juices from the food we cook (instead of tossing them aside like with boiling), while we dramatically enhancing the absorption of nutrients like beta-carotene.

However you slice it,
cooking has played a significant role
in human history, perhaps influencing
how our anatomy and physiology have changed.
It has certainly improved the digestibility
of our food by literally doing some of the
work necessary to break down
whole food into its constituent
chemical parts.

RECIPES

Breakfast

Soups and Stews

Main Dishes

Side Dishes

Desserts

BREAKFAST

Tools:

· parchment paper	bowl
· medium skillet	· knife
· peeler	· whisk
· medium	· cutting board

Serves: 4-6

Prep Time: 10 minutes

Cook Time: 2 hours on low

1 large, orange sweet potato/yam

1 pound Italian sausage

1 cup sliced mushrooms

½ cup fresh spinach leaves

12 eggs

Salt and pepper to taste

Sausage, Mushroom, & Spinach Crock-tata

This dish is perfect for busy people and fancy enough to be served for brunch or a special occasion. I like to make this recipe on Sundays because there is enough left over for our early morning workdays. It's so nice to have breakfast ready without the need to wake up the rest of the house from banging around in the kitchen.

1. Line your slow cooker with parchment paper.

2. Peel the sweet potato, and slice thinly. Line the bottom of the parchment-covered slow cooker with the sweet potato slices.

3. In a medium-sized skillet, brown the sausage until fully cooked. Discard the grease, and evenly spread the cooked sausage in the slow cooker on top of the sliced sweet potatoes.

4. Thinly slice one cup of fresh mushrooms, and layer the mushrooms evenly over the top of the sausage.

5. Wash the spinach, drain it, and layer the spinach leaves evenly on top of the mushrooms.

6. In a medium-sized bowl, whisk the eggs together. Pour the eggs evenly over the top of the sausage, mushrooms, and spinach in the slow cooker.

7. Cover and cook on low for two hours. Check with a toothpick at one and one-half hours to be sure to avoid over-cooking. Salt and pepper to taste.

Parchment Paper Tip:

How to line your slow cooker with parchment paper:
1) Tear off a piece of parchment paper that is slightly bigger than the top of your slow cooker. 2) Cut the parchment paper starting at the corner cutting towards the center of the paper. In each corner make about a 4-6 inch long cut. (Note this will vary depending on the size and shape of your slow cooker). 3) After cutting all four corners, lay the parchment paper over the top of your slow cooker. Press the parchment paper down into the base of the stoneware. You may have to cut a little more of the paper to get it to lay flat. 4) Fold/crease the paper to smooth out the edges of the parchment paper. Trim the edges of the parchment paper if you have a lot of excess paper hanging over the top to ensure that the lid will fit correctly on the slow cooker.

Serves: 4-6

Prep Time: 10 minutes

Cook Time: 2 hours on low

1 sweet potato/yam, shredded

1 cup ham, diced (pre-cooked)

½ cup bell pepper, diced

¼ cup onion, diced

10 eggs

Denver-Style Frittata

Remove the cheese in this American classic breakfast, and you can easily make it a Paleo favorite. Cooking breakfast in the slow cooker is extremely helpful for those busy mornings. I love to make a slow cooker breakfast to not only minimize time spent in the kitchen, but to minimize the mess as well! Kayden likes to help me add all the ingredients, and he's even becoming an expert at spreading the sweet potatoes on the bottom of the slow cooker.

1. Line your slow cooker with parchment paper (see tip on page 60).

2. Peel one sweet potato, and shred it in a food processor. Spread the shredded sweet potato evenly on the bottom of the parchment-lined slow cooker to create a "crust."

3. Spread the diced ham evenly on top of the shredded sweet potatoes.

4. Layer the diced bell pepper and onion evenly on top of the ham.

5. In a medium-sized bowl, whisk eggs together. Pour the egg mixture evenly over the top of the bell pepper, onion, and ham.

6. Cook on low for two hours. Check with a toothpick after one and one-half hours to avoid over-cooking.

Note:

Use the leftover Slow Cooked Ham
found on page 126 to save time
and minimize waste!

Recipe Notes

· parchment paper	· blade
· peeler	· knife
· food processor with shred	· cutting board
	· medium skillet

Serves: 4-6

Prep Time: 15 minutes

Cook Time: 2 hours on low

1 sweet potato/yam, shredded

3-4 pieces of bacon

1-2 links of Italian Sausage, casing removed

3 mushrooms, sliced

¼ cup onion, diced

¼ cup bell pepper, diced

10-12 eggs

Kitchen Sink

When I was growing up in the small town of Red Bluff, my dad occasionally took me to a little breakfast place that served a dish called "The Kitchen Sink." It contained almost everything you could imagine, which was then added to eggs. One morning I had quite a few leftovers lingering in my refrigerator, so I decided to throw "the kitchen sink" into my slow cooker ... figuratively speaking, of course. This tasty creation was the result. Feel free to add or substitute ingredients to your liking.

1. Line your slow cooker with parchment paper (see tip on page 60).

2. Peel the sweet potato, and shred it using your food processor's shred attachment. Spread the shredded sweet potato evenly over the bottom of the slow cooker.

3. Cut the bacon strips into smaller bite-sized chunks, and cook them in a skillet on medium heat until browned. If you are using pre-cooked bacon, crumble it into small pieces. Sprinkle the bacon evenly over the sweet potato.

4. With the casing removed from the sausage, crumble it into a skillet, and cook thoroughly over medium heat. Spread the cooked sausage evenly over the bacon and sweet potato.

5. Evenly spread the mushrooms, onion, and bell pepper on top of the sausage in the slow cooker.

6. Beat the eggs together until smooth, and pour them evenly over the mixture in the slow cooker.

7. Cover, and cook on low for two hours. To avoid over-cooking, remove the mixture immediately by carefully lifting the parchment paper out of the slow cooker.

Tips:

If I make this recipe to eat throughout the week, I usually cook it on a Sunday afternoon. To save time, I cook extra bacon and sausage for breakfast so that all of those ingredients are ready when I start my slow cooker.

Jalapeño Sausage Hash

Serves: 4

Prep Time: 10 minutes

Cook Time: 6-8 hours on low

3 medium sweet potatoes, peeled and shredded

1 red bell pepper, diced

1 cup yellow onion, diced

1 jalapeño pepper, diced

1 pound of sausage, chopped

Garnish with avocado (optional)

My husband is not an egg lover, so this is a spicy, egg-free dish that we created together. It's now one of his favorites. One perk with this dish is that you can start it at night before you go to bed and wake up to a warm, ready-to-eat breakfast. If you like eggs, like me, you can add a fried egg to the top right before serving.

1. Peel the sweet potatoes, and shred them in a food processor using the shredding blade. Then, place the sweet potatoes in the slow cooker.

2. Add the diced bell pepper, onion, and jalapeño pepper to the slow cooker.

3. Chop the sausage into bite-sized pieces, and add them to the slow cooker. If using ground sausage be sure to brown the sausage before adding it to your slow cooker

4. Cover, and cook on low for six to eight hours.

Note:

This dish can also be easily cooked on the stovetop by using a little coconut oil in the pan.

Recipe Notes

Sun-Dried Pesto Frittata

Serves: 4-6

Prep Time: 10 minutes

Cook Time: 2 hours on low

2 small zucchini squash, shredded

10-12 eggs

½ of a 12-ounce jar of whole sun-dried tomatoes, packed in olive oil

4-6 tablespoons homemade pesto

- Pesto Ingredients -

4 cloves of garlic

1 cup basil leaves, packed and stems removed

½ cup walnut oil (or olive oil)

¼ juice of large lemon

Salt and pepper to taste

The first time I made this frittata was for the Fragoso family! I knew they had a busy week ahead, so I surprised them with this frittata. The Fragoso kids reported back that this was one of the best frittatas they had ever had. Now, I often make it for my own family, and we always enjoy this twist on the classic. Feel free to substitute black olives or bell peppers for the sun-dried tomatoes for a variation that nicely complements the tasty pesto.

1. Line the bottom of your slow cooker with parchment paper (see tip on page 60).

2. In a food processor, use the shredding blade to shred the zucchini squash. Then, place the squash in the bottom of the slow cooker.

3. Beat the eggs until they are mixed well. Pour the egg mixture on top of the shredded zucchini.

4. Evenly place the sun-dried tomatoes and pesto on top of the egg mixture. Feel free to use more or less to your liking.

5. Cover, and cook on low for two hours.

Pesto

1. Place garlic, basil, oil, and lemon juice in a food processor or blender, and blend until smooth and creamy. Be sure to stop and scrape the sides periodically to ensure that all of the basil is blended.

2. Add salt and pepper to taste.

Recipe Notes

Tools:

· measuring cup	· peeler
· measuring spoon	· knife
	· cutting board

Serves: 4-6

Prep Time: 5 minutes

Cook Time: 6 hours on low

2 apples, peeled and shredded

3 cups almond meal

3 cups water

1 tablespoon cinnamon

Slow Cooked Almond Apple Cereal

While growing up, my mother frequently made us Cream of Wheat and oatmeal for breakfast. If you are craving one of those old-time favorites, this cereal is a great substitute. I enjoy it with a splash of coconut milk and honey served alongside my bacon and eggs.

1. Peel and shred the apples, and place them in the slow cooker.

2. Add all of the remaining ingredients, and stir well.

3. Cover and cook on low for six hours.

Recipe Notes

SOUPS
AND
STEWS

Prep Time: 5 minutes

Cook Time: 12-24 hours (the longer the better)

2 pounds bones (beef, lamb, turkey, chicken, or fish)

12 cups cold water (preferably filtered)

1 tablespoon vinegar (balsamic, red wine, or apple cider)

Sea salt (optional)

Kelp powder (optional)

Benefits of Bone Broth

· *Full of minerals*
· *Great for gut health*
· *Healing for the adrenals*
· *Contains gelatin (great for hair and nails)*

SOUPS AND STEWS

Bone Broth

If there is one recipe that merits dedicating an entire slow cooker to it around the clock, it's bone broth. It's one of the simplest things to make, and it's also one of the most nutritious. Plus, you'll never need to buy chicken or beef stock again! I usually use the carcass of a roasted chicken, but you can use the bones and cartilage of any meat—beef, lamb, turkey, or fish. Adding vinegar helps extract the minerals from the bones, and it will keep five to seven days in the refrigerator. You can also freeze it for use several months later.

1. Place the bones in the slow cooker.

2. Add the cold, filtered water, making sure to completely cover the bones.

3. Add the vinegar.

4. Cover and set slow cooker on high, bringing to a boil.

5. Turn the slow cooker to low for at least twelve hours. When cook time is completed, remove or strain the bones from the broth. The bones should be very soft.

Note:

Before serving, add a pinch of sea salt and kelp powder to improve both the flavor and iodine content.

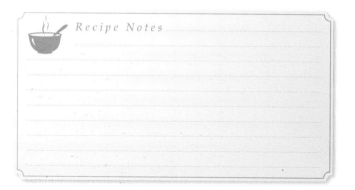

Recipe Notes

Prep Time: 10 minutes

Cook Time: 8-10 hours on low

1 leftover carcass from a whole chicken (page 164)

2 cups water

Salt and pepper to taste

Slow Cooked Chicken Stock

While I know it's easy to buy chicken stock, there's something to be said for making your own. Use the carcass from my whole chicken recipe found on page 164 to make your own stock, which can be used in many of my slow cooked recipes.

1. Place the leftover carcass into the slow cooker.

2. Add the water, salt, and pepper to the slow cooker. Cover, and cook on low for eight to ten hours. Remove or strain the bones from the stock.

Recipe Notes

Tools:	
· cutting board	· garlic crusher
· measuring spoons	· knife

Serves: 6-8

Prep Time: 5 minutes

Cook Time: 8 hours on low

2 cinnamon sticks, whole

4 pounds boneless leg of lamb

1 medium yellow onion, chopped

4 medium carrots, chopped

1 tablespoon cumin

1 tablespoon coriander

1 teaspoon cayenne pepper

2 tablespoons fresh ginger, minced, or 1 teaspoon dried ginger

4 garlic cloves, minced

Nicki's Indian Lamb Stew

As you now know, my husband is not an adventurous eater, so lamb is not something I prepare in our home. But my sister and Robb love lamb, and they love Indian food, too. This is one of their staple slow cooked dishes. Luckily, Costco sells imported grass-fed leg of lamb from Australia at a great price. This dish is full of flavor and is wonderful to come home to, especially on a cold winter day. It makes enough for a couple to eat for two or three days, or it's great for a dinner night with friends.

1. Place the cinnamon sticks on the bottom of the slow cooker.

2. Place the lamb in the slow cooker on top of the cinnamon sticks.

3. Chop the onion and carrots, and place them on top of the lamb in the slow cooker.

4. Mince the garlic and ginger, and add them to the slow cooker.

5. Add the remaining spices.

6. Cover and cook on low for eight hours.

Recipe Notes

Tools:

· cutting board
· knife
· can opener
· measuring
· cup
· measuring spoons
· food processor

Chipotle Chicken Stew

Serves: 4

Prep Time: 15 minutes

Cook Time: 4-6 hours on low

2 marinated chicken breasts, cut approximately 1" thick (see marinade recipe that follows)

2 tablespoons coconut oil

1 medium onion, coarsely diced

1 turnip, cut into approximately ¾-inch squares

1 rutabaga, cut into approximately ¾-inch squares

1 cup winter squash (acorn or butternut), cut into approximately ¾-inch squares

1 14.5-ounce can diced tomatoes, juice and all

3 cups organic chicken broth

2 teaspoons Penzeys Galena Street Rib and Chicken Rub Spice, or Chico Rub found on page 236

1 tablespoon dried basil

½ teaspoon ground ancho chili pepper

This recipe was given to me by a very special client, Laura, who not only generously shares her amazing garden fresh vegetables with my family, but also her warmth and passion in the kitchen. This is a great recipe to prep at night, and then in the morning toss everything together in the slow cooker.

1. Marinate the chicken breasts overnight.

2. The next day, place the coconut oil in the slow cooker.

3. Chop the onion, and place in the bottom of the slow cooker.

4. Cut the turnip, rutabaga, and butternut squash into ¾-inch squares, and spread them evenly on top of the onion.

5. Cut the chicken, and place it on top of the vegetables. Discard the marinade.

6. Add the rest of the ingredients, cover, and cook on low for four to six hours.

- Marinade -

1. In a food processor, blend the following ingredients:

   2 to 3 chipotle peppers in adobo sauce (3 for a spicier marinade)

   3 cloves garlic

   ¼ cup honey

   1 tablespoon ground mustard

   1 teaspoon chili powder

   2 tablespoons apple cider vinegar

   1 8-ounce can tomato sauce

   ½ teaspoon sea salt

   ½ teaspoon fresh ground pepper

Tools:

· cutting board	· measuring cups
· knife	· measuring spoons
· can opener	

Serves: 6-8

Prep Time: 20 minutes

Cook Time: 6-8 hours on low

2 tablespoons olive oil

1 yellow sweet potato, diced

1 cup carrots, diced

2 celery stalks, diced

2 zucchini squash, diced

2 shallots, diced

2 cloves of garlic, minced

28 ounces chicken or vegetable broth

28-ounce can of organic diced tomatoes with juice

¼ cup fresh kale, chopped

¼ cup fresh spinach leaves

2 bay leaves

2 teaspoons oregano

1 teaspoon basil

1 teaspoon parsley

¼ teaspoon cayenne pepper

¼ teaspoon Penzeys Mural of Flavor, or Garden Rae found on page 236

Traditional Minestrone Soup

This soup has been a long-time favorite of mine. By omitting the beans and pasta and making a few minor tweaks, I created a very hearty and tasty version of minestrone. This recipe fills the house with mouthwatering aromas and is sure to warm and comfort you on a cold day.

1. Place the olive oil in the bottom of your slow cooker.

2. Peel and dice the sweet potato and add to the slow cooker.

3. Dice the carrots, celery, zucchini, and shallots, and spread them evenly over the sweet potato.

4. Mince the garlic, and add to the slow cooker mixture.

5. Add the chicken or vegetable broth, followed by the tomatoes with juice.

6. Wash and chop the kale, removing the spine, and add to the slow cooker.

7. Next, add the spinach.

8. Add all remaining ingredients.

9. Give the entire mixture a few good stirs, cover, and cook on low for six to eight hours.

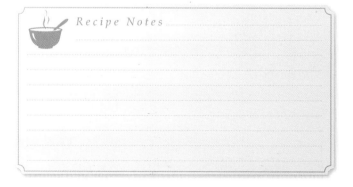

Recipe Notes

Tools:

- cutting board
- knife
- measuring cups
- blender or food processor
- can opener

Serves: 4

Prep Time: 25 minutes

Cook Time: 6-8 hours on low

2 large orange sweet potatoes or yams, fully-cooked (page 204)

2-3 boneless, skinless chicken breasts

1 small yellow onion, chopped

2 carrots, chopped

3-4 celery stalks, chopped

2 tablespoons butter or olive oil

2 cups chicken broth or stock

2 jalapeño peppers, diced

½ cup coconut milk

Jalapeño Sweet Potato Chowder

This recipe is what I call a husband pleaser! The creaminess of the coconut milk and the richness of the sweet potato make it a total comfort food. Feel free to omit the chicken and turn it into a side dish for Aunt Robin's Roast (page 140), or use pork loin instead of chicken. This recipe can be cooked all day in your slow cooker, or it can be prepared on the stovetop in a fraction of the time.

1. Cook the sweet potatoes the night before, and store them in the refrigerator.

2. The next day, rinse (and trim if necessary) the chicken breasts, and place them in the bottom of the slow cooker.

3. Chop the onions, carrots, and celery into even bite-sized pieces.

4. Place the vegetables in a medium-sized skillet with butter or olive oil, and sauté over medium heat until the onions are translucent. Then, add them to the slow cooker.

5. Scoop out the cooked sweet potato insides, and place them in a blender with one cup of the chicken broth or stock. Purée until smooth, and add to the slow cooker.

6. Cut the stems off of the jalapeño peppers, and slice them lengthwise. Remove and discard the seeds, dice them, and add them to the slow cooker.

7. Add the coconut milk and the remaining chicken broth to the slow cooker, and stir well.

8. Cover and cook on low for six to eight hours.

9. Uncover, and cook for another half hour. This will thicken the chowder considerably.

To cook on your stovetop:

1. Omit the boneless, skinless chicken breast, and use a fully-cooked rotisserie chicken.

2. Follow the above instructions, but cook in a soup pot.

3. Bring to a boil, and simmer for twenty minutes.

4. Add the fully-cooked rotisserie chicken, and simmer for an additional ten minutes.

Stuenkel Stew

Tools:
- cutting board
- knife
- measuring spoons

Serves: 4-6

Prep Time: 8 minutes

Cook Time: 8-10 hours on low

4-6 pounds chuck roast

2 tablespoons Penzeys Galena Street Rib Rub, or Chico Rub found on page 236

Salt and pepper to taste

1 medium yellow onion, chopped

4-5 celery stalks, chopped

1 leek, chopped

6-8 mushrooms, chopped

1 large can crushed tomatoes

1 tablespoon red pepper flakes

3 cloves garlic, minced

1 bay leaf

This recipe is not only simple, but also tasty and hearty. It is not your standard beef stew, as the red pepper flakes give it a nice kick. Kayden enjoys this recipe as is, but for those who prefer a more traditional stew or a milder flavor, omit the red pepper flakes or try my Old Fashioned Beef Stew recipe (page 88).

1. Season the roast generously with salt, pepper, and Galena Street Rub. Then, place the roast in the slow cooker.

2. Evenly chop the onion, celery, leek, and mushrooms, and add them to the slow cooker.

3. Add the crushed tomatoes, red pepper flakes, garlic, and bay leaf.

4. Cover and cook on low for eight to ten hours.

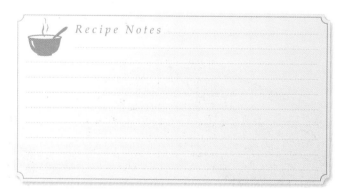

Recipe Notes

Old Fashioned Beef Stew

Serves: 6-8

Prep Time: 10 minutes

Cook Time: 4-6 hours on low, then 2-3 hours on high

2-3 pounds lean stew meat, cut into 1-inch pieces

1 quart beef broth

1 teaspoon celery salt

½ teaspoon thyme

½ teaspoon basil

1 teaspoon parsley

1 teaspoon marjoram

2 cloves garlic, minced

1 medium yellow onion, chopped

1 cup carrots, chopped

1 cup celery, chopped

2 cups sweet potatoes (yellow), peeled and diced

1 cup mushrooms, chopped

1 16-ounce can diced tomatoes

This is my favorite throwback to beef stew, as it is simple and classic. You can enjoy this dish as a stand-alone meal or serve it on top of my Garlic Mashed Sweet Potatoes recipe (page 214) for an even heartier meal.

1. Place the stew meat, beef broth, celery salt, and herbs in your slow cooker.

2. Mince the garlic, and evenly chop the onion, carrots, and celery. Add them to the slow cooker.

3. Cover, and cook on low for four to six hours.

4. Peel and dice the sweet potato, and chop the mushrooms. Add both to the slow cooker after the first four to six hours of cooking.

5. Add the diced tomatoes, cover, and cook on high for another two to three hours.

Note:

If there is too much liquid to your liking, simply remove the lid for the last twenty minutes of cooking so that some of the liquid evaporates.

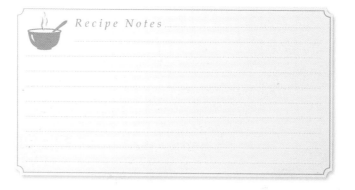

Recipe Notes

Tools:
· cutting board
· knife
· can opener
· measuring cups
· measuring spoons

Serves: 6-8

Prep Time: 30 minutes

Cook Time: 6 hours on low

½ pound bacon, cooked and diced

1 yellow onion, diced

3 garlic cloves, minced

5 celery stalks, diced

6 carrots, diced

5 large carrots, diced

2 14.5-ounce cans diced tomatoes with juice

4 cups chicken broth

2 teaspoons oregano

1 teaspoon thyme

⅛ teaspoon cayenne pepper

½ cup fresh parsley, diced

10 ounces clams, drained

8 ounces clam juice

Salt and pepper to taste

Manhattan Clam Chowder

After going Paleo, I thought I would never be able to enjoy clam chowder again. That is, until I remembered the tomato-based Manhattan Clam Chowder! This is my version of the popular soup. It really does satisfy the taste buds and is not complicated to make.

1. Cook the bacon in a large soup pot.

2. Add the onion, and cook until translucent.

3. Add the garlic, celery, and carrots, and sauté for three to four minutes. Turn off the heat, and set aside.

4. In the slow cooker, add the tomatoes, chicken broth, spices, and parsley, and mix well.

5. Add the bacon and vegetable mixture to the slow cooker, turn it on low, and cook for six hours.

6. Add the clams and clam juice, and heat for another ten minutes or just until the clams are warm.

7. Season with salt and pepper to taste, and serve.

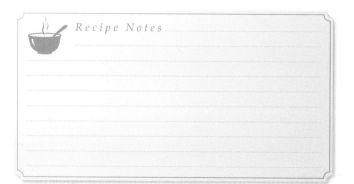
Recipe Notes

Tools:
- cutting board
- knife
- can opener
- measuring
- cup
- measuring spoons
- garlic crusher

Serves: 4-6

Prep Time: 10 minutes

Cook Time: 6 hours on low

3 pounds boneless, skinless chicken breasts or thighs

½ yellow onion, chopped

3 cloves garlic, crushed

1 can bamboo shoots, drained

1 can sliced water chestnuts, drained

1½ tablespoons rice vinegar

2 tablespoons wheat-free tamari or coconut aminos

1 teaspoon sesame seed oil

2 teaspoons hot chili oil

2 tablespoons lemon juice

2 Portobello mushrooms, sliced

2 cups chicken stock

1 cup water

Hot and Sour Soup

This spicy soup is a great starter for my Asian Chicken Wraps (page 168). I make it with chicken to please my husband, but you can easily use pork or add shrimp to it just before serving. You can use less chili oil if you prefer less spicy soup, or more vinegar and lemon if you prefer a more sour soup.

1. Place the chicken into the slow cooker.

2. Evenly chop the onion into bite-sized pieces, and place the onion over the chicken.

3. Using a garlic crusher, crush the garlic into the slow cooker.

4. Drain the water from both the bamboo shoots and the water chestnuts, and add them to the slow cooker.

5. Add the remaining ingredients, cover, and cook on low for six hours.

Note:

*This recipe can be easily adapted for the stovetop.
In a large soup pot, sauté the onion and garlic in the sesame oil
until translucent. Add the remaining ingredients
and bring to a boil. Then, cover and simmer
for another thirty minutes.*

Recipe Notes

· medium
  sauté pan
· cutting
  board
· knife

· measuring
  spoons
· measuring
  cup

Serves: 4-6

Prep Time: 10 minutes

Cook Time: 8-10 hours on low

1 medium yellow onion, chopped

4 celery stalks, chopped

3 carrots, chopped

2 tablespoons olive oil

4 boneless, skinless chicken
breasts (or fully-cooked rotisserie
chicken)

2 garlic cloves, minced

1 jalapeño pepper, diced

16 ounces chicken broth

1 14.5-ounce can diced tomatoes
with green chilies

1 28-ounce can of El Pato
Enchilada sauce

1½ teaspoon cumin

1½ teaspoon chili powder

½ cup coconut milk

Tortilla-less
Chicken Soup

This soup recipe is my husband's favorite. In fact, I think I made
this soup for him almost every week this past winter. It can be
slow cooked all day or made in about thirty minutes if you use a
pre-cooked rotisserie chicken. This recipe does have a mild kick
to it, but even Kayden enjoys the spice as is.

1. In a medium-sized pan, sauté the onion, celery, and carrots in
   olive oil until onions are translucent (three to five minutes over
   medium heat).

2. Place the sautéed vegetables in the slow cooker.

3. Rinse and trim the chicken breast (if necessary), and add it to the
   slow cooker. (If using pre-cooked chicken, do not add it to the slow
   cooker until the last twenty minutes of cooking.)

4. Add the remaining ingredients to the slow cooker, stir, cover, and
   cook on low for eight to ten hours.

Recipe Notes

Tools:

- large soup pot
- ladle or large slotted spoon
- food processor or blender
- can opener

Serves: 4-6

Prep Time: 15 minutes

Cook Time: 6-8 hours on low

8 large fresh tomatoes

½ yellow onion, minced

2 cloves garlic, minced

16 ounces chicken stock or broth

1 can coconut milk

Salt and pepper to taste

Creamy Tomato Soup

One of my husband's favorite childhood meals was grilled cheese and tomato soup. Well, I don't have an answer for the grilled cheese, but I do have a great Paleo-friendly recipe for homemade tomato soup. This recipe is husband-approved and sure to bring back those childhood memories.

1. Place the tomatoes in a large soup pot, and fill the pot with water so that all of the tomatoes are covered. Bring to a boil for five to ten minutes until the skin starts to crack. Remove from heat.

2. Using a ladle or slotted spoon, carefully remove the tomatoes from the water, peel the skin off of the tomatoes, and place them in a food processor.

3. Add the onion and garlic to the food processor, and purée until smooth.

4. Place the tomato, onion, and garlic mixture in your slow cooker.

5. Add the coconut milk, chicken stock, salt, and pepper to the slow cooker, and stir.

6. Cover, and cook on low for six to eight hours.

Recipe Notes

Serves: 4-6

Prep Time: 10 minutes

Cook Time: 6-8 hours on low

4 cups butternut squash, peeled and cubed

½ onion chopped

3 stalks celery, chopped

3-4 carrots, chopped

32 ounces chicken stock or broth

Salt and pepper to taste

Hearty Butternut Squash Soup

This recipe is my spin on the traditional puréed butternut squash soup. The hearty vegetables and the richness of the butternut squash make this soup very versatile. Serve as a starter for any meal or you can add chicken to turn it into a main dish. If you prefer more of the traditional puréed style soup, place it in the blender after it is cooked.

1. Peel the butternut squash, and cut it in half lengthwise. Scoop out the seeds, cube the squash, and add it to the slow cooker. (Or use butternut squash that has already been cubed.)

2. Chop the onions, celery, and carrots, and add them to the slow cooker.

3. Add the chicken broth, cover, and cook on low for six to eight hours.

4. Add salt and pepper to taste.

Recipe Notes

Serves: 4-6

Prep Time: 5 minutes

Cook Time: 8 hours on low

3 pounds (approximately) chuck roast

1 tablespoon garlic powder

Salt and pepper to taste

1 quart organic beef broth

1 bag frozen green beans

1 bag frozen carrots

1 bag frozen pearl onions

Lazy Man's Chuck Roast Stew

This dish is the ultimate easy meal that is virtually idiot-proof. All of these ingredients were purchased at Trader Joe's and can be combined in your slow cooker in less than five minutes, delivering a tasty and hearty stew just eight hours later.

1. Place the meat in your slow cooker, and season it with the garlic powder, salt, and pepper.

2. Add the beef broth and all of the frozen vegetables to the slow cooker.

3. Cover, and cook on low for eight hours.

Recipe Notes

· cutting board
· large soup pot
· knife
· whisk
· measuring spoons
· measuring cups

Coconut Cream of Broccoli Soup

Serves: 6-8

Prep Time: 20 minutes

Cook Time: 6-8 hours on low

1 medium yellow onion, diced

4-5 celery stalks, diced

2 cloves garlic, diced

3 tablespoons butter, ghee, or coconut oil

3 tablespoons coconut flour

1 can coconut milk

2 cups chicken broth

¼ teaspoon Penzeys Mural of Flavor, or Garden Rae found on page 236

5 cups broccoli florets

Salt and pepper to taste

This recipe was inspired by my husband, who absolutely loves Cream of Broccoli Soup. The coconut milk is the perfect substitution for the cream, as it does not have an overpowering coconut flavor and provides the creaminess you want.

1. Dice the onion, celery, and garlic, and place them in a large soup pot with 1 tablespoon of butter.

2. Sauté the onion, celery, and garlic over medium heat until onions are translucent.

3. Place the mixture in your slow cooker.

4. Return the soup pot to the heat, and melt the remaining two tablespoons of butter over medium heat. Once the butter is melted, add the coconut flour one tablespoon at a time. Stir constantly using a whisk to ensure that there are no lumps. It should look like a thick paste once all of the coconut flour has been added to the butter.

5. Add the coconut milk to the paste, and stir frequently. It should be thick and creamy.

6. Pour the coconut milk mixture into the slow cooker.

7. Add the chicken broth and spices.

8. Add the broccoli florets to the slow cooker.

9. Cover and cook on low for six to eight hours.

Recipe Notes

Classic Chicken Soup

Tools:
- cutting board
- knife
- can opener
- measuring cup
- measuring spoons

Serves: 4-6

Prep Time: 10 minutes

Cook Time: 8-10 hours on low

4-6 boneless, skinless chicken breasts or thighs

6 carrots, chopped

5 celery stalks, chopped

1 small onion, chopped

½ head cauliflower florets

28 ounces chicken broth

1 teaspoon Penzeys mural of flavor, or Garden Rae found on page 236

Salt and pepper to taste

This is one of Kayden's favorite soups! It warms my heart when he asks me for this slow cooked Chicken Soup. I usually have Kayden help me chop the vegetables and put them into the slow cooker, which may be in part why he loves this soup so much.

1. Place the chicken in the slow cooker.
2. Chop the carrots, celery, and onion into bite-sized pieces, and place them on top of the chicken in the slow cooker.
3. Cut the cauliflower into florets, and place them in the slow cooker.
4. Add the chicken broth and seasonings to the slow cooker.
5. Cover and cook on low for eight to ten hours.

Recipe Notes

Tools:

- cutting board
- knife
- measuring cup
- measuring spoons
- food processor

Serves: 4-6

Prep Time: 5 minutes

Cook Time: 6-8 hours on low

1 yellow onion, diced

3 garlic cloves

2 cups strained tomatoes

½ cup beef broth

2 tablespoons chili powder

1 tablespoon ground cumin

1 tablespoon oregano

⅛ teaspoon cayenne pepper

1 tablespoon red wine vinegar

Sea salt to taste

4 pounds beef stew meat

South of the Border Beef Stew

This beef stew is versatile. You can make it a brand new meal by simply changing the spices. For example, leave out the chili powder and cumin and replace them with Italian seasoning for an Italian beef stew. Feel free to add diced carrots, celery, or chunks of sweet potatoes for a heartier meal.

1. In a food processor, add the onion, garlic, strained tomatoes, beef broth, spices, and vinegar. Blend until smooth.

2. Place the stew meat in the slow cooker, and add the sauce. Mix well.

3. Cover, and cook on low for six to eight hours.

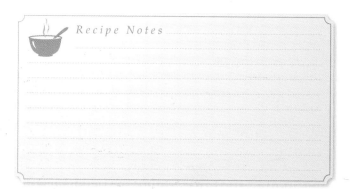

Recipe Notes

MAIN
DISHES

Tools:

- food processor
- large mixing bowl
- spatula
- measuring spoons and cup

Serves: 4

Prep Time: 15 minutes

Cook Time: 4 hours on high

½ head cauliflower, finely chopped

1 garlic clove, finely chopped

¼ yellow onion, finely chopped

1 pound grass-fed ground beef

½ cup fire-roasted salsa (I used Trader Joe's Brand)

1 small can of fire-roasted diced green chilis

1 egg

½ cup almond flour

2½ teaspoons chili powder

¾ teaspoon cumin

¾ teaspoon oregano

¼ teaspoon basil

5 tablespoons organic tomato paste

Salt and pepper to taste

Fire-Roasted Meatloaf

I have never really been a big fan of meatloaf; my past meatloaf experiences were just plain boring. Since I know it's a staple on most family menus, though, I set out to create a healthy, but livelier version. The result is this meatloaf, which is great right out of the slow cooker, and the flavors are even better as leftovers for lunch the next day!

1. Using a food processor, finely chop the cauliflower, garlic, and onion and set aside.

2. In a large mixing bowl, combine the ground beef, salsa, chilis, and egg.

3. Add the cauliflower, garlic, and onion mixture to the beef mixture.

4. Add the almond flour and spices to the beef mixture. Using your hands, kneed and mix all of the ingredients together.

5. Shape the beef mixture into a loaf and place it in the slow cooker.

6. Using a spatula, evenly spread the tomato paste on top of the meatloaf.

7. Cover, and cook on high for four hours or until the internal temperature of the meatloaf has reached 160°F. Salt and pepper to taste.

Recipe Notes

Boneless Pork Ribs

Tools:

- large skillet
- tongs
- measuring spoons and cup
- cutting board
- medium bowl or square baking dish

Serves: 6

Prep Time: 25 minutes

Cook Time: 4-6 hours on low

2½-3 pounds boneless country style ribs

5 tablespoons coconut oil

½ yellow onion, chopped

2 red apples, chopped

½ cup fresh pineapple, chopped (optional)

Salt and pepper to taste

- Rub Ingredients -

½ cup coconut flour

2 teaspoons dried ground mustard

1 teaspoon Penzeys Galena Street Rib Rub, or Chico Rub found on page 236

1 teaspoon chipotle powder

2 tablespoons crushed red chili peppers

These ribs are not only melt-in-your-mouth tasty, but extremely easy to prepare. You can enjoy them as is or top them with your favorite Paleo or gluten free barbecue sauce. I really enjoy this dish served over my Cauliflower Fried Rice (page 184). I'm sure this meal will become a family favorite in your home just as it is in ours!

1. Rinse and pat the pork dry, sprinkle with a little salt, and set aside.

2. In a medium bowl or square baking dish, sift all of the rub ingredients together until well mixed.

3. Melt the coconut oil over medium-high heat in a large skillet.

4. Using tongs, carefully coat all sides of one rib evenly with the rub mixture.

5. Place the coated rib into the skillet, and brown on all sides.

6. Repeat steps 4 and 5 until all of the pieces of pork have been evenly coated with the rub and browned.

7. Place the browned ribs into the slow cooker.

8. Chop the onion and apples into ¾-inch pieces, and spread them evenly on top of the ribs in the slow cooker.

9. For a sweeter taste, add the pineapple on top of the apples and onions.

10. Cover, and cook on low for four to six hours.

11. Add salt and pepper to taste, and serve.

Recipe Notes

Serves: 4-6

Prep Time: 15 minutes

Cook Time: 4-6 hours on low

2 tablespoons olive oil

1 cup carrots, chopped
(about 2-3 small carrots)

1 cup yellow onion, chopped
(about ½ onion)

1 cup zucchini, chopped
(about 2-3 small zucchini)

1 bell pepper, chopped
(I used green)

2 cups mushrooms, sliced

1 pound grass-fed ground beef

1 pound Italian sausage,
casing removed

28 ounces organic crushed
tomatoes

28 ounces whole peeled
tomatoes with juice

2 large cloves of garlic, crushed

2 tablespoons dried oregano or
4 tablespoons fresh oregano

1 tablespoon dried basil or
2 tablespoons fresh basil

1 tablespoon garlic pepper

Spaghetti with Meat Sauce

This recipe might seem basic, but simple is sometimes better. In fact, one of the very first meals that my husband made for me early in our relationship was a version of this sauce (see note below). You can add or omit ingredients to your liking, so it's versatile. It's great over your favorite noodle replacement; we like to alternate between spaghetti squash, zucchini noodles, and even sautéed spinach.

1. Place the olive oil into the bottom of the slow cooker, and turn the slow cooker on low.

2. Chop the carrots, onion, zucchini, and bell pepper into ¾-inch pieces. Add the vegetables to the slow cooker.

3. Slice the mushrooms, and place them in the slow cooker.

4. In a large skillet, brown the beef and pork on medium-low heat so that there is just a hint of pink left. Watch carefully to avoid overcooking. Add the partially cooked beef and sausage to the slow cooker.

5. Add all of the remaining ingredients to the slow cooker, and give it a few stirs.

6. Cover, and cook on low for four to six hours.

Note:

*You can also substitute cubed boneless, skinless chicken breasts
for the beef and pork to add a different twist.
While I prefer coming home to spaghetti sauce
that has been cooking all day, you can also prepare this
on your stovetop. To do so, sauté the vegetables in a large pot
until tender. Brown the beef and pork in a separate pan
until they are no longer pink, and add them to the pot of vegetables.
Add the remaining ingredients, bring it to a boil,
and simmer for thirty minutes.*

Tools:

- small mixing bowl or saucer
- cutting board
- knife
- measuring spoons
- measuring cup

Serves: 4-6

Prep Time: 10 minutes

Cook Time: 4-6 hours on low

4-5 pounds beef brisket
(I used bottom cut)

1 medium yellow onion, sliced
into rings

½ cup water

- *Rub Mixture -*

2 tablespoons garlic pepper

2 teaspoons onion powder

2 teaspoons ground mustard

1 teaspoon garlic powder

1 teaspoon Penzeys Old World
Seasoning, or Cobblestone found
on page 237

2 teaspoons salt

Beef Brisket Sandwich

Sometimes, you just want a sandwich. Back in our pre-Paleo days, my husband consumed more than his fair share of sandwiches, so he was my inspiration for this recipe. This is the perfect weekend lunch with friends and family, especially with my Sweet Potato Chips (page 206).

1. Trim the fat down to ¼-inch on the brisket.

2. Combine all of the rub ingredients into a small mixing bowl or saucer.

3. Coat both sides of the brisket with the rub.

4. Slice the onion into small even rings, and place them in the bottom of the slow cooker.

5. Place the rub-coated brisket on top of the onions.

6. Add the water to the slow cooker.

7. Cook on low for four to six hours or for two hours on high. Check the progress halfway through to avoid over-cooking. The meat should reach 160°F in the thickest part.

8. Prepare the Sweet Potato Chips (page 206).

9. Place the brisket between two pieces of Sweet Potato Chips, and enjoy your sandwich.

Note:

*This recipe is also great with Grandpa's BBQ Sauce (page 188).
I also like to caramelize onions and add them
to the Brisket Sandwich.*

Recipe Notes

Mild Yellow Chicken Curry

Serves: 5

Prep Time: 15 minutes (with kids, 30 minutes)

Cook Time: 4 hours on high or 6-8 hours on low

2 tablespoons olive oil

6 celery stalks, chopped

5 medium carrots, chopped

1 medium yellow onion, chopped

1 medium sweet potato, peeled and chopped

3 pounds (about 12-15) boneless, skinless chicken thighs

1 13.5-ounce can of coconut milk

½ cup chicken broth or stock

3 tablespoons yellow curry

This is one of our family's favorite meals—a mild and simple curry. If you want to spice it up a bit, add some fresh cracked pepper or garlic pepper. My husband prefers his curry spicier, while our 3-year-old enjoys this meal without the added kick. Feel free to tinker and adjust the flavors to fit your family. Incidentally, it's great over a bed of Cauliflower Rice (page 182).

1. Pour the olive oil into the bottom of the slow cooker.
2. Chop the celery, carrots, and onion, and place them in the slow cooker.
3. Peel and chop the sweet potato, and add it on top of the vegetables.
4. Rinse the chicken thighs, and add them to the slow cooker.
5. Add the coconut milk and chicken broth.
6. Stir in the curry powder.
7. Cover, and cook on high for four hours or on low for six to eight hours.

Note:

Be sure to check for and remove any bones or bone fragments when rinsing the chicken thighs.

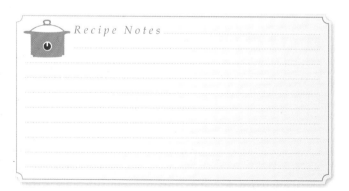
Recipe Notes

Tools:
- cutting board
- food processor or blender
- spatula
- measuring spoons and cup

Serves: 4-6

Prep Time: 15 minutes

Cook Time: 4 hours on high

1 tablespoon olive oil

6-8 boneless, skinless chicken thighs

4 cloves garlic

1 cup basil leaves, packed and stems removed

½ cup walnut oil (or extra virgin olive oil)

¼ of a large lemon, juiced

Pesto Chicken

Pesto has always been one of my husband's favorites, and after going Paleo, we have discovered that pesto tastes amazing on foods besides plain old pasta. I like this dish for several reasons, but more than anything, I enjoy doubling the pesto recipe to use for other dishes like on top of my eggs in the morning or over hamburgers. I'll also sometimes make a double batch of the entire meal so that we have leftovers for lunch throughout the week. Of course, it's great over my Spaghetti Squash (page 220).

1. Add the olive oil to the bottom of slow cooker.

2. Rinse the chicken thighs, and remove any remaining bones. Place them in the slow cooker.

3. Add the garlic, basil, walnut oil, and lemon juice to a food processor or blender, and blend until smooth. Be sure to stop and scrape the sides periodically to ensure all of the basil is blended. This makes about ¾ cup of pesto.

4. Add salt and pepper to taste.

5. Pour the pesto mixture over the chicken thighs in the slow cooker.

6. Cook on high for four hours or until the chicken is thoroughly cooked and no longer pink inside.

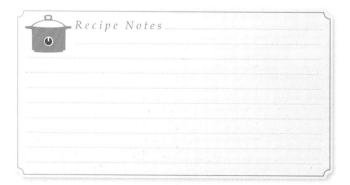

Recipe Notes

Tools:

· roasting pan or baking sheet
· food processor
· cutting board
· large skillet
· large bowl

Serves: 4-6

Prep Time: 45 minutes

Cook Time: 6-8 hours on low

2-4 pounds pork shoulder (I used pork country style boneless ribs)

2 teaspoons salt

10 medium/large tomatillos

2 poblano peppers

2 jalapeño peppers

3 serrano peppers

4 large cloves garlic, unpeeled

½ cup coconut flour, sifted

½ cup coconut oil (may need a little more/less depending on the amount of pork used)

1 bunch cilantro

2 cups chicken stock

Slow Cooked Chili Verde

This dish is great any time of the year or any meal of the day. You can enjoy it by the bowl full, on top of your favorite salad, or even on top of your eggs. The combination of the peppers and garlic give it a warm and authentic flavor you are sure to love.

1. Cube the pork into one-inch cubes, and place them in a bowl. Sprinkle with salt, and set aside.

2. Remove and discard the husks from the tomatillos, wash the tomatillos with warm water, and cut them in half.

3. Wash the peppers, and place them with the tomatillos and unpeeled garlic on a roasting pan or baking sheet. Broil on high for seven minutes or until blackened. Watch them carefully and turn them halfway through the broiling process.

4. Sift the coconut flour into a large bowl. Working in batches, thoroughly coat the pork with the coconut flour. (You may need more or less flour depending on the amount of pork used.)

5. In a large skillet, melt the coconut oil over medium-high heat. Brown the pork in the skillet, and set the meat aside.

6. Place the blackened peppers aside to cool. Purée the tomatillos and garlic together, and pour the mixture into your slow cooker.

7. Add the browned pork to the slow cooker on top of the tomatillo/garlic purée.

8. Peel the skins off of the poblano peppers, and remove the seeds and stems. Then, place the peppers in a food processor.

9. Cut the stems off of the jalapeño and serrano peppers, and add them to the food processor.

10. Add the cilantro, and blend all of the ingredients together. This should look more like a paste when it is blended.

11. Add the chicken stock to the slow cooker, and give the mixture a few stirs.

12. Cook on low for six to eight hours.

Note:

Depending on the peppers, this recipe can pack some heat. Be sure to taste it before serving. If it is too hot, add one to two red tomatoes to counter the spiciness of the jalapeño and serrano peppers.

Mild Shredded Chicken

Serves: 4-6

Prep Time: 10 minutes
(even for my husband)

Cook Time: 4 hours on low

4-6 boneless, skinless chicken breasts

2 small cans El Pato Jalapeño Salsa Sauce (green can)

This is the easiest dish to make in this entire cookbook! My husband jokes that it is easier to make than Top Ramen, but it's much better for you, of course! You can enjoy it by itself, over a salad (which is my favorite), or wrapped in lettuce and topped with your favorite salsa. I'm sure this will become one of your go-to meals, thanks to its simplicity.

1. Place the chicken breasts in the slow cooker, and pour the sauce over them.

2. Cover, and cook on low for four hours.

Note:

*If there is a lot of liquid remaining in your slow cooker,
remove the lid, and continue to cook for another twenty minutes or so.
Some of the liquid will evaporate and thicken.*

Recipe Notes

Slow Cooked Ham

Serves: 10-12

Prep Time: 10 minutes

Cook Time: 8 hours on low

4-6 pounds ham, bone-in optional (I used locally raised organic Llano Seco Pork)

Whole cloves (many)

¹/₈ cup + 2 tablespoons pineapple juice

3 tablespoons orange juice

2 tablespoons maple syrup

My grandfather on my mother's side made a ham every time we visited. I'd help him cover it with an abundance of cloves and help mix his sugar concoctions to baste over the meat. None of his hams ever tasted the same, but they were all fantastic. I wanted to recreate the essence and flavors of my grandfather's ham, and this recipe is the result. It will not only fill your house with an amazing aroma, but will leave you with a meal to fill your belly for a few days.

1. Decorate your ham by inserting as many whole cloves as you like into it. This is a great job for your little helpers.

2. Place the ham in the slow cooker fat side down, and pour the pineapple juice and orange juice over the top.

3. Drizzle the ham with the maple syrup.

4. Cover, and cook on low for eight hours or until the internal temperature of the ham reaches 160°F. If you are using a pre-cooked/smoked ham, place it in the slow cooker until the internal temperature reaches 140°F.

Note:

*Depending on the size and shape of your slow cooker,
you may have to shave down your ham for it to fit.
You can either fit the shaved-off pieces on the sides of your ham
or save them for breakfast.*

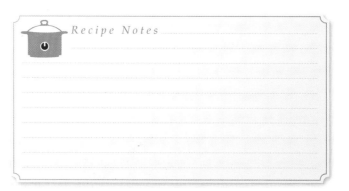

Recipe Notes

Chicken Cacciatore

Tools:

- cutting board
- knife
- measuring cup
- measuring spoons

Serves: 6-8

Prep Time: 20 minutes

Cook Time: 6-8 hours on low or 3-4 hours on high

1 large onion

3 pounds chicken, cut up, or 4 legs and 4 thighs

1 16-ounce can organic diced tomatoes

1 8-ounce can organic tomato sauce

1 cup mushrooms, chopped

2-3 cloves garlic

2 teaspoons fresh oregano, diced

½ teaspoon fresh basil, diced

1 bay leaf

¼ cup dry white wine

Salt and pepper to taste

This is a Paleo-fied version of Chicken Cacciatore from the original recipe given to me by my Aunt Linda. The mild yet savory flavor is suitable for the whole family. You can enjoy it over squash or sweet potatoes.

1. Thinly slice the onion, and place it in the bottom of your slow cooker.

2. Place the chicken on top of the onion, and add the diced tomatoes and tomato sauce.

3. Chop the mushrooms, and add them to the slow cooker.

4. Dice the garlic, oregano, and basil, and place them on top of the mushrooms.

5. Add the bay leaf, wine, and salt and pepper to your liking.

6. Cover, and cook on low for six to eight hours or on high for three to four hours.

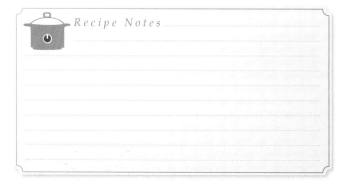

Recipe Notes

MAIN DISHES

Serves: 4

Prep Time: 8 minutes

Cook Time: 2-4 hours on low

1 pound grass-fed ground beef

1 bell pepper, diced
(I used yellow)

½ yellow onion, diced

2 celery stalks, diced

1 8-ounce can tomato sauce

1 6-ounce can tomato paste

½ teaspoon Penzeys California
Pepper (optional)

1½ teaspoons ground mustard

¼ teaspoon ground ancho chile
pepper

½ teaspoon chili powder

¼ teaspoon salt

1 teaspoon maple syrup

¼ teaspoon Penzeys Arizona
Dreaming, or Fiery Sunset found
on page 236

¼ teaspoon Penzeys BBQ 3000,
or Summer Blaze found on page
237

Sloppy Joes

Parents who are trying to convert their families to Paleo often ask me, "What about the kid-friendly foods we used to eat?" This recipe brings me back to my own childhood and is sure to satisfy your kids. They taste great and are a fun and messy sandwich when you place the mixture between Sweet Potato Chips (page 206).

1. Brown the ground beef in a skillet over medium-high heat (about five minutes), and place the browned beef in your slow cooker.

2. Dice the bell pepper, onion, and celery, and place them on top of the beef in the slow cooker.

3. Add the remaining ingredients and spices to the slow cooker.

4. Stir, cover, and cook on low for two to four hours.

Recipe Notes

Tools:

- soup pot
- cutting board
- knife
- large skillet
- measuring cup
- measuring spoons
- food processor or blender

Serves: 4-6

Prep Time: 20 minutes

Cook Time: 6-8 hours on low

3 tomatillos

2 serrano peppers

1 jalapeño pepper

1 medium yellow onion, chopped

1 bell pepper, chopped

1 pound beef chuck, cubed

1 pound grass-fed ground beef

1 28-ounce can crushed tomatoes

1 28-ounce can diced tomatoes

1 teaspoon ground ancho chili pepper

1 teaspoon chili powder

1 teaspoon chipotle powder

2 teaspoons cumin

1 teaspoon red chili pepper, flakes

1 teaspoon garlic powder

¼ cup olive oil

¼ cup beef stock

3 tablespoons tomato paste

2 tablespoons Penzeys Chili 9000, or Kicking Chili found on page 237

Chili with a Kick

Chili is an essential year-round staple. This main dish will warm you up during cold winter months, or you can enjoy it as a side dish at a summertime gathering. This recipe has even passed my picky husband's standards.

1. Pull the husks off of the tomatillos. In a small pot, bring the tomatillos, serrano peppers, and jalapeño pepper to a boil. Continue boiling until they are tender, drain, and remove from the heat.

2. Chop the onion and bell pepper.

3. Cube the beef chuck if it is not pre-cubed.

4. In a large skillet, brown the cubed beef chuck in two tablespoons of olive oil or coconut oil, and place it in the slow cooker.

5. Using the same skillet, brown the ground beef with the onion and the bell pepper. Remove it from the heat.

6. Using a food processor or blender, blend the tomatillos, serranos, jalapeño, ancho chili pepper, chipotle powder, cumin, red chili peppers, garlic powder, chili powder, and olive oil together until smooth. Stir the seasoning mixture into the ground beef mixture.

7. Add the ground beef with spices to the slow cooker.

8. Add the remaining ingredients (beef stock, tomato paste, crushed tomatoes, diced tomatoes, and Penzeys Chili 9000) to the slow cooker. Stir, cover, and cook on low for six to eight hours.

Recipe Notes

Tools:

- large soup pot
- large skillet
- cutting board
- knife
- peeler
- spoon
- ladle

Serves: 4-6

Prep Time: 45 minutes

Cook Time: 4-6 hours on low

2 tablespoons olive oil

1 cup carrots, chopped
(about 2-3 small carrots)

1 cup yellow onion, finely
chopped (about ½ onion)

1 cup zucchini, finely chopped
(about 2-3 small zucchini)

2 cups sliced mushrooms

1 bell pepper, diced (I used green)

1 pound grass-fed ground beef

1 pound Italian sausage

28 ounces organic crushed
tomatoes

28 ounces whole peeled
tomatoes with juice

2 large cloves garlic, crushed

2 tablespoons dried oregano or
4 tablespoons fresh oregano

1 tablespoon dried basil or
2 tablespoons fresh basil

1 tablespoon garlic pepper

1 butternut squash

Butternut Squash Lasagna

Just because you eat Paleo, primal, or gluten free, you don't have to miss out on traditional family meals like lasagna! This recipe has the same flavors that you find in the standard dish, but instead of grain-based noodles, it uses nutritious butternut squash. This surprising combination has received rave reviews from friends and family alike.

1. Place olive oil into the bottom of a large soup pot on medium heat.

2. Add the carrots, onions, zucchini, mushrooms, and bell peppers, and sauté until the vegetables are tender.

3. While the vegetables are cooking, brown the beef and sausage on medium heat in a separate skillet until fully cooked.

4. Add the cooked beef and sausage mixture to the vegetables in the soup pot.

5. Add the remaining ingredients except for the butternut squash, mix well, and simmer for thirty minutes.

6. While the sauce simmers, peel, halve, and scoop out the seeds of the butternut squash. Cut the cleaned squash lengthwise in one-quarter to one-half-inch thick strips resembling thick lasagna noodles. They don't have to be perfect; remember that it's a casserole. You could also cut the squash into semicircles if you prefer.

7. In the slow cooker, ladle in a layer of the meat sauce, then evenly spread the squash slices on top of the meat sauce. Continue to alternate meat sauce and squash slices until you have reached at least four layers or more. Fewer layers run the risk of burning.

8. Cover, and cook on low for four to six hours.

Recipe Notes

Grandpa's BBQ Beef

Tools:

- airtight container
- small bowl
- measuring spoons

Serves: 6-8

Prep Time: 5 minutes + marinate overnight

Cook Time: 3-4 hours on low

3 pounds brisket

2 ounces Liquid smoke (make sure it is gluten free)

1 tablespoon garlic salt

1 tablespoon celery salt

1 tablespoon onion salt

Grandpas BBQ Sauce (page 188)

This is a meal that my Grandpa always made during the summer months, but he slow cooked the BBQ Beef in the oven rather than in a slow cooker. We always looked forward to get-togethers when Grandpa would make this dish, and I'm honored to be able to recreate this family favorite to share with all of you! I hope this meal gives you many memories of joy and happiness with your loved ones, as it has for our family.

1. Pour the liquid smoke over both sides of the brisket.

2. In a small bowl, combine the garlic salt, celery salt, and onion salt, and mix well. Sprinkle both sides of the meat with the salt mixture.

3. Wrap or seal the brisket in an airtight container, and refrigerate overnight.

4. Next day, place the brisket in the slow cooker, cover, and cook on low for three to four hours.

5. Make Grandpa's BBQ sauce (page 188).

6. When the beef is done, shred it using two forks.

7. Turn the slow cooker to the warm setting, stir in the sauce, and serve.

Recipe Notes

Serves: 4-6

Prep Time: 5 minutes

Cook Time: 2-4 hours on low

2-3 pounds beef cut into fajita strips

2-3 tablespoons red curry paste

1 can coconut milk

1 tablespoon red pepper flakes

Red Beef Curry

This is a great go-to meal when you don't have a lot of time to prep. This recipe is simple, yet it will taste like you labored over it for hours. Serve it with sautéed broccoli or over Cauliflower Rice (page 182) for a well-rounded, nutritious meal.

1. Place the beef strips into the slow cooker.

2. Stir in the red curry paste (3 tablespoons if you like it spicier).

3. Add the coconut milk and red pepper flakes.

4. Stir, cover, and cook on low for two to four hours.

Recipe Notes

Aunt Robin's Roast

Tools:
- cutting board
- measuring spoons
- measuring cup
- knife

Serves: 4-6

Prep Time: 15 minutes

Cook Time: 8-10 hours on low

3-4 pounds pot roast

7 celery stalks, chopped

1 medium yellow onion, chopped

40-50 baby carrots, whole
(or 3-5 regular carrots, chopped)

½ cup vegetable stock

1 tablespoon of garlic salt

2 tablespoons of Worcestershire sauce

1 tablespoon pepper

1 teaspoon salt (or to taste)

This version of pot roast comes from my husband's sister. She usually makes it during our holiday stay with her, and it's a family favorite. I also love having the leftovers from this roast for lunch the next day.

1. Place the roast in your slow cooker.

2. Chop the celery and onion, and add them to the slow cooker.

3. Add the carrots, vegetable stock, and remaining seasonings.

4. Cover, and cook on low for eight to ten hours.

Recipe Notes

- medium skillet
- cutting board
- knife
- food processor
- kitchen shears
- measuring cup

Serves: 4-6

Prep Time: 40 minutes

Cook Time: 4 hours on high

½ pound Italian pork sausage, casings removed

2 cups mushrooms, finely chopped

2 green onions, diced

1 head cauliflower, finely chopped

4-6 small artichokes

1 lemon, cut into wedges

1 cup water

Stuffed Artichokes

This recipe is one of my personal favorites to enjoy as a main or side dish, depending on the size of the artichoke and your appetite. The prep for this meal might be a bit more labor-intensive, but the end result is well worth the effort. This lesson also applies to life in general.

1. Crumble the pork sausage into a medium skillet, and brown over medium heat until fully cooked. Set aside.

2. Finely chop the mushrooms, and dice the green onions.

3. Cut the cauliflower into florets, and process them in a food processor until they are finely chopped.

4. In a small mixing bowl, add the cauliflower, chopped mushrooms, green onions, and cooked sausage, and mix well to make the stuffing.

5. To prepare your artichokes, cut off the stem, and use kitchen shears to cut off the spiny tip of each leaf. Pull back all of the leaves as much as possible until you get to the center of the artichoke, and pull out the smaller yellow leaves until you get to the heart. Scrape the furry inside of the artichoke out, leaving the heart intact.

6. Wash the artichoke and squeeze lemon juice into the leaves and center.

7. Stuff the center of each artichoke with as much stuffing as possible.

8. Place each stuffed artichoke into the bottom of the slow cooker, and add one cup of water to the bottom of the slow cooker.

9. Cover, and cook on high for four hours.

Recipe Notes

Serves: 6-8

Prep Time: 20 minutes
+ marinate overnight

Cook Time: 6 hours on low

2 cups freshly squeezed orange
juice

4 tablespoons maple syrup

2 tablespoons orange zest

6-8 thick pork loin chops

2 tablespoons coconut oil

2 cups mushrooms, sliced

Orange Maple Glazed Pork Chops

The pork chops marinate overnight, so all you have to do in the morning is pop them in the slow cooker and walk out the door! I suggest serving these with my Roasted Brussels Sprouts (page 196).

Marinade Instructions:

1. In a medium-sized mixing bowl, whisk together the orange juice, maple syrup, and orange zest until well mixed.

2. Reserve half of the marinade in a separate container for glazing, and store it in the refrigerator.

3. Put the pork chops and the other half of the marinade in a large zip lock bag or other airtight container, and marinate the meat overnight in the refrigerator.

Cooking Instructions:

1. Remove the marinated pork chops from the refrigerator.

2. Melt the coconut oil in a medium-sized saucepan on medium-high heat.

3. Sear the pork chops until brown on both sides, and place the seared pork chops in your slow cooker.

4. Cover, and cook on low for six hours.

5. Prior to serving, bring the reserved half of the marinade to a slow boil in a medium-sized sauté pan, stirring frequently.

6. Add the sliced mushrooms to the sauté pan, and turn the heat down. Simmer for three to five minutes or until the mushrooms are tender. Remove from heat.

7. Plate the pork chops, and drizzle the mushrooms and glaze over the top.

Note:

*You can also cook these pork chops in the oven or on the grill.
To cook in the oven, sear them and bake in an oven-safe pan
at 350°F for 30 minutes. To grill, place them on the grill
for about 8 minutes on each side.*

Recipe Notes

NorCal Margarita Chicken

Serves: 6-8

Prep Time: 5-10 minutes + marinate overnight

Cook Time: 6 hours on low or 3-4 hours on high

Juice and zest of 1 lime

¾ teaspoon cumin

½ teaspoon chili powder

2 cloves garlic, crushed

1 tablespoon tequila

8-10 chicken thighs

This recipe is a tribute to Robb Wolf's NorCal Margarita. If cooked in a slow cooker, it's great served over roasted vegetables or a salad with a little extra squeeze of fresh lime and olive oil. What I love most about this recipe is that it can also be prepared on the grill and ready to eat in just minutes. There's nothing like grilled margarita chicken, a big green salad, and a NorCal Margarita on a hot summer day!

1. Combine all of the ingredients in an airtight/leak-proof container or bag, and mix well so that the chicken is thoroughly covered in the marinade. Then, leave it in the refrigerator overnight.

2. Next day, place the chicken into your slow cooker, taking care not to pour in all of the remaining marinade.

3. Cover, and cook on low for six hours.

Recipe Notes

Lemon Herb Pork Loin

Serves: 6-8

Prep Time: 5 minutes
+ marinate overnight

Cook Time: 7-9 hours on low

Juice and zest of 1 lemon

4 cloves garlic, crushed

¼ cup olive oil

2 sprigs fresh rosemary

2 pork loins (about 2-4 pounds)

This recipe is perfect for anyone who likes to prep the night before, which leaves very little work in the morning. I have served it at dinner parties to rave reviews. Enjoy it with a salad or with my Stuffed Artichoke recipe (page 142).

1. Combine all of the ingredients in an airtight container or leak-proof bag, and marinate the pork overnight in the refrigerator.

2. Next day, place the pork in your slow cooker.

3. Cover and cook on low for seven to nine hours.

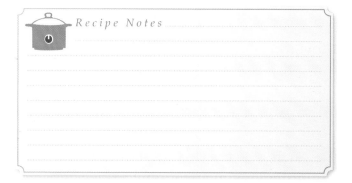

Recipe Notes

Grandpa's Saucy Ribs

Tools:

· none

Serves: 4-8

Prep Time: 5 minutes

Cook Time: 4 hours on high or 8 hours on low

2-3 racks of baby back pork ribs (cut as needed to fit into your slow cooker)

Salt and pepper

Grandpa's BBQ Sauce (page 188)

This is another wonderful recipe that was passed down to me from my Grandpa, and it is easy and delicious. Be sure to have plenty of Grandpa's BBQ Sauce made and ready for days when you have only a few minutes to throw something in the slow cooker, like these scrumptious ribs!

1. Rinse and pat the ribs dry. If necessary, cut them to fit in your slow cooker.

2. Generously sprinkle all sides of the ribs with salt and pepper.

3. Cover, and cook on high for four hours or on low for eight hours.

4. When the ribs are thoroughly cooked, turn the slow cooker to warm, and add Grandpa's BBQ sauce.

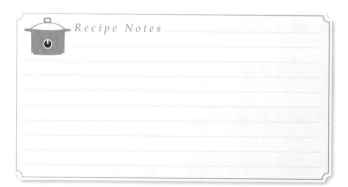

Recipe Notes

Herb Rubbed Turkey Breast

Serves: 4-6

Prep Time: 5 minutes

Cook Time: 8 hours on low

½ teaspoon sage, fresh

1 teaspoon thyme, fresh

¼ teaspoon celery salt

1 sprig rosemary

Salt and pepper to taste

3-5 pounds turkey breast, bone in or boneless

Who says you have to wait until November to have the aromas of Thanksgiving fill your house? This recipe is simple enough to start in the morning so that you can come home from work to a healthy and tasty meal. Pair it with my Garlic Mashed Sweet Potatoes (page 214) and Roasted Brussels Sprouts (page 196) for a well-rounded Paleo meal.

1. Combine the herbs in a small bowl, and mix well.

2. Rub the herb mixture generously over the outside of the turkey breasts and under the skin, taking care not to tear the skin.

3. Place the turkey breasts in your slow cooker, cover, and cook on low for eight hours.

Note:

You can also prepare this dish in the oven. To do so, place the turkey breasts in an oven-safe dish, and bake at 350°F for twenty minutes per pound or until the internal temperature of the meat reaches 160°F.

Recipe Notes

Serves: 8-10

Prep Time: 5 minutes

Cook Time: 4-6 hours on low

Chicken wings,
1st and 2nd sections

1 5-ounce jar Tabasco brand
buffalo style hot sauce

Slow Cooked
Buffalo Wings

When preparing for the NorCal Strength and Conditioning annual Paleo potluck event, I wanted to contribute something a little different. So I came up with the idea of buffalo wings, which was quickly shot down by one of our local butchers. He claimed that the bones would fall apart in a slow cooker. Being told "no" has never stopped me before, so I was determined to make it work. The result is a ridiculously easy recipe with only two ingredients. The butcher was wrong!

1. Place the chicken wings in your slow cooker.

2. Cover, and cook on low for four to six hours. Cooking time will vary depending on how full you fill your slow cooker with the chicken. Be sure to check on the meat every few hours to avoid over-cooking.

3. Once the chicken wings are fully cooked, cover the wings with the Tabasco buffalo style hot sauce. Stir them to coat evenly with the sauce.

4. Turn the slow cooker to warm, and serve.

Note:

*If you prefer crispier wings, simply pop them in the oven
at 375°F.*

Recipe Notes

Carne Asada

Serves: 4-6

Prep Time: 5 minutes

Cook Time: 8-10 hours on low

Our family absolutely loves Mexican food, and this recipe is as simple and tasty as they come. It's perfect for the delicate palate of a child, but feel free to put your own spin on it to suit your taste. We often enjoy this dish on top of Simple Cabbage and Cilantro Salad (page 208), or you can serve it in a lettuce wrap topped with fresh squeezed lime juice.

1 tablespoon garlic pepper

1 teaspoon garlic salt

½ teaspoon onion powder

½ teaspoon ancho chili powder

½ teaspoon cumin

½ teaspoon adobo seasoning

2 teaspoons salt

2-3 pounds flank steak

1. In a small bowl, combine the garlic pepper, garlic salt, onion powder, ancho chili powder, cumin, adobo seasoning, and salt. Generously coat all sides of the flank steak with the seasoning mixture.

2. Place the seasoned flank steak into your slow cooker, cover, and cook on low for eight to ten hours. Then, shred the meat prior to serving.

Recipe Notes

Chipotle Meatballs

Serves: 4-6

Prep Time: 30 minutes

Cook Time: 6-7 hours on low

- Meatballs -

1 pound ground beef

1 pound ground pork

2 teaspoons sea salt

2 teaspoons oregano

½ teaspoon chipotle powder

2 egg yolks

Cilantro for garnish

- Sauce -

1 small yellow onion, chopped

3 garlic cloves, minced

2 cups tomato sauce

1 cup beef broth

¼ teaspoon chipotle powder

2 tablespoons honey

1 teaspoon oregano

Sea salt and pepper to taste

These meatballs are savory, subtly spicy, and scrumptious! Anytime I make meatballs, Kayden loves to help. Make extra for leftovers, and enjoy these the next day for lunch. We often eat these meatballs with my Spaghetti Squash (page 220) or a big green salad.

1. In a medium-sized mixing bowl, thoroughly mix together all of the meatball ingredients with your hands, and set aside.

2. Add the onion, garlic, tomato sauce, and beef broth to your slow cooker, and mix well.

3. Add the honey and spices, and whisk together.

4. Form the meat mixture into meatballs that are just larger than a golf ball. Gently drop each meatball into the sauce in the slow cooker.

5. Cover, and cook on low for six to seven hours. Serve garnished with cilantro.

Recipe Notes

Cajun Veggies with Grilled Shrimp

Tools:
- knife
- cutting board
- BBQ or grill

Serves: 4

Prep Time: 10 minutes + grill time

Cook Time: 4 hours on low

1 red pepper sliced in chunks (not diced)

1 green pepper (can throw in some yellow for added color too) sliced in chunks (not diced)

2 medium yellow onions, sliced

3-4 zucchini, cut in ¼-inch wheels

½ teaspoon crushed red Italian pepper

2 cans stewed tomatoes (Cajun or Italian herbed are best)

8-12 jumbo shrimp

2 tablespoons olive oil

2 tablespoons cajun seasoning

Salt and pepper to taste

This dish is perfect when you want a "light meal" or need a side. Though the shrimp are not cooked in the slow cooker, it takes just minutes to grill them.

1. Cut the peppers into thick slices, and chop them further into bite-size chunks. Place the peppers in your slow cooker.

2. Cut the onions in half, and slice them evenly. Add the onions to the slow cooker.

3. Slice the zucchini into ¼-inch wheels, and add them over the onions.

4. Add the crushed red pepper and stewed tomatoes.

5. Cover, and cook on low for four hours.

For Shrimp:

1. Clean and peel the shrimp.

2. Drizzle them with olive oil and cajun seasoning.

3. Grill the shrimp over medium heat until they are thoroughly cooked. (They should turn pink).

Recipe Notes

Serves: 4

Prep Time: 10 minutes

Cook Time: 4 hours on high

2-3 small acorn squash

1 pound mild Italian pork sausage

1 cup onion, diced

2 cups mushrooms, chopped

2 cups spinach leaves

1 cup water

Stuffed Acorn Squash

This is a deceiving dish, as it doesn't look like something you would usually prepare in a slow cooker. But the squash hold their shape and cook beautifully, leaving you with a comforting and warm meal that reminds me of a fancier version of Shepherd's pie. This dish can be enjoyed as a main dish or side. It has a delicate flavor that is suitable for all ages.

1. Place 1 cup of water in the bottom of your slow cooker.

2. Cut the acorn squash in half lengthwise, remove the seeds, and set aside.

3. In a large skillet, brown the Italian sausage over medium heat.

4. Add the onion, mushrooms, and spinach to the sausage, and cook for one to two minutes. Remove from the heat.

5. Stuff the cavity of the halved acorn squash with as much of the sausage and vegetable mixture as you can. It's okay to overstuff them.

6. Carefully place the squash in the slow cooker, and repeat this process for each halved squash.

7. Cover, and cook on high for four hours.

Note:

This recipe can also be made in the oven.
Follow the slow cooker steps, but place in an oven-safe baking dish.
Bake at 350°F for fifty minutes.

Recipe Notes

Serves: 4

Prep Time: 5 minutes

Cook Time: 4–5 hours on high or 8 hours on low

1 whole, free range chicken, giblets removed

Salt and pepper to taste

Slow Cooked Whole Chicken

This is the easiest way to cook a whole chicken. It's tasty with just the salt and pepper, or spice it up with the seasoning of your choice. Occasionally, I add a little Cajun seasoning to mine. This dish is also the base from which I make Chicken Stock (page 76).

1. Remove the giblets and innards from the chicken. Rinse and pat the chicken dry.

2. Place the chicken in your slow cooker.

3. Generously sprinkle salt and pepper on the outside and inside the cavity of the chicken.

4. Cover, and cook on high for four to five hours or on low for eight hours.

Note:

*You will know the chicken is done
when the meat falls off the bone.
This recipe can also be made in the oven.
Prepare the chicken as you would for a slow cooker,
but place it in an oven-safe dish.
Bake at 350°F on the center rack for twenty minutes
per pound or until the internal breast temperature
reaches 165-175°F.*

Recipe Notes

Fire-Roasted Pork Loin

Serves: 4-6

Prep Time: 5 minutes

Cook Time: 8 hours on low

1 large pork loin or 2 small pork tenderloins

1 bag frozen fire-roasted bell peppers and onions

14.5-ounce can organic diced and fire-roasted tomatoes with green chilis

1 cup chicken broth

Salt and pepper to taste

I love meals that are fast to prep but still always please! If you like pork loin in the slow cooker, you'll love this meal because the smokiness of the fire-roasted bell peppers and onions really kicks the flavors up a notch. Sometimes, the simplest meals are the most flavorful.

1. Place the pork loin in your slow cooker, and season it with salt and pepper to taste.

2. Add the fire-roasted bell peppers, onions, fire roasted tomatoes, and chicken broth.

3. Cover, and cook on low for eight hours.

Recipe Notes

Asian Chicken Wraps

Serves: 4-6

Prep Time: 15 minutes

Cook Time: 4-6 hours on low

4 boneless, skinless chicken breasts

1 can water chestnuts, sliced

1 can bamboo shoots, chopped

8 mushrooms, chopped

3 garlic cloves, minced

1 tablespoon wheat-free tamari or coconut aminos

1 tablespoon honey

1 tablespoon rice vinegar

2 teaspoons Asian chili pepper sauce or oil

1 teaspoon sesame seed oil

1 bunch green onions

1 head iceberg lettuce

This dish is light enough for lunch or dinner. You can wrap the chicken lettuce, or for a more "burrito" type feel, there is a great product called coconut wraps made by Pure Wraps. Either way you wrap it, this dish is sure to please.

1. Cube the chicken breasts into one-inch cubes, and place them into your slow cooker.

2. Drain, and slice the water chestnuts. Then, add them to the slow cooker.

3. Drain, and chop the bamboo shoots. Then, spread them evenly on top of the water chestnuts.

4. Chop the mushrooms, and mince the garlic. Spread them evenly on top of the bamboo shoots.

5. Add the remaining ingredients except for the green onions and the lettuce.

6. Cover, and cook on low for four to six hours or until the chicken is thoroughly cooked.

7. Serve in lettuce wraps, and garnish with green onions.

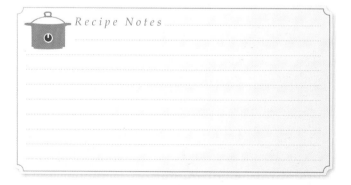
Recipe Notes

BBQ Apple Chicken

Serves: 4-6

Prep Time: 5 minutes

Cook Time: 7-8 hours on low

6-8 boneless, skinless chicken thighs

2 apples, peeled and chopped

1 yellow onion, chopped

1 clove garlic, minced (optional)

- BBQ Sauce-

1 cup organic ketchup

⅛ cup prepared mustard

⅛ cup honey (optional)

½ tablespoon allspice

Pinch of cayenne (optional)

I must give credit for this dish to my sister in law, Robin, who was kind enough to share it with us. The ingredients are simple, affordable, and easy to find. It has been a savior for those long busy days.

1. Place the chicken thighs in your slow cooker.

2. Peel and chop the apples.

3. Chop the onion, and mince the garlic.

4. Add the apples, onion, and garlic to the slow cooker.

5. Combine all of the BBQ sauce ingredients in a small bowl and stir well. Pour the BBQ sauce in the slow cooker, cover, and cook on low for seven to eight hours.

Recipe Notes

Chili Beef Short Ribs

Serves: 4-6

Prep Time: 5 minutes

Cook Time: 8 hours on low

1 can tomato sauce

½ onion

2 tablespoons chili powder

2-3 garlic cloves

1 teaspoon ground pepper

1 tablespoon balsamic vinegar

1 tablespoon honey

1 tablespoon ground mustard

3-4 pounds short ribs

Short ribs in the slow cooker are nothing less than fall-off-the-bone perfection, and it's almost torture to smell these as you wait for them to finish cooking. Nevertheless, the wait is worth it. Another bonus of this recipe is how easy it is to make. I usually plan it for hectic days when I can quickly pop these in the slow cooker during breakfast.

1. Combine all ingredients except the meat in a blender or food processor and purée.

2. Place the ribs in your slow cooker, and pour the blended mixture over them.

3. Cook on low for eight hours.

Recipe Notes

Beef Shoulder Roast

Serves: 4-6

Prep Time: 5 minutes

Cook Time: 8 hours on low

1 can El Pato Jalapeño Salsa Sauce (small can)

1 can diced green chilis

1 tablespoon cumin

½ onion

1 tablespoon garlic powder

1 can tomato sauce

3-4 pounds beef shoulder

This recipe is fabulous for cold winter nights. I often bake sweet potatoes to go with it, and everyone is happy with plenty of leftovers for the next day. Be sure to always have staple ingredients handy like diced green chilis and El Pato sauce for quick meal prep.

1. Combine all ingredients except the meat in a blender, and purée.

2. Place the beef in your slow cooker, and pour the blended mixture over it.

3. Cook on low for eight hours.

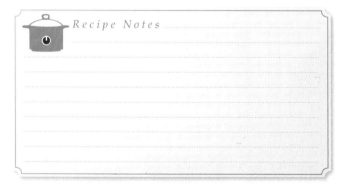

Recipe Notes

- knife
- cutting board
- lime squeezer
- measuring spoon
- measuring cup

Serves: 4-6

Prep Time: 10 minutes

Cook Time: 4 hours on high

1 small yellow onion, sliced

1 bell pepper, sliced

3 limes

3-4 pounds of chicken (breasts, thighs, or legs)

4 tablespoons Trader Joe's taco seasoning mix (or the taco or fajita seasoning of your choice)

¼ cup chicken stock or broth

Fiesta Lime Chicken

I love coming home to a house filled with the aroma of a fiesta. The flavors of this dish resemble that of fajitas. You can enjoy it by itself, on top of my Simple Cabbage and Cilantro Salad (page 208), or fajita style in lettuce wraps.

1. Thinly slice the onions and bell pepper into strips, and place them in your slow cooker.

2. Cut one lime in half, and squeeze the juice over the onion and bell pepper strips.

3. Place the chicken on top of the onion and bell pepper strips, and evenly sprinkle them with two tablespoons of the taco seasoning.

4. Turn the chicken over, and sprinkle the remaining two tablespoons of seasoning on them.

5. Squeeze the remaining two limes over the chicken, and add the chicken broth to the slow cooker.

6. Cover, and cook on high for four hours.

Recipe Notes

Serves: 4-6

Prep Time: 15 minutes

Cook Time: 6-8 hours on low

4-6 pieces of cooked bacon, crumbled

4-6 boneless, skinless chicken breasts

1 cup organic cherry tomatoes, halved

1 cup fresh basil

Salt and pepper to taste

Bacon Bruschetta Stuffed Chicken Breasts

I love the flavors and textures that come together in this dish. The basil and tomatoes take me back to high school when I traveled to Italy. My husband likes it topped with my homemade Pesto (page 68).

1. In a large skillet, cook the bacon until it is thoroughly done. Crumble the bacon, and set it aside.

2. Butterfly each chicken breast by cutting them in half lengthwise and keeping one side intact.

3. Evenly stuff the chicken breasts with the tomatoes, basil, and bacon.

4. Fasten the open side of the stuffed chicken breasts with toothpicks to hold them closed.

5. Place the stuffed chicken breasts into your slow cooker, cover, and cook on low for six to eight hours.

6. Season the dish with salt and pepper to taste.

Recipe Notes

SIDE DISHES

Serves: 4

Prep Time: 5 minutes

Cook Time: 10 minutes

1 head cauliflower

2 tablespoons butter or coconut oil

Cauliflower Rice

Hands down, this simple and easy recipe is the best rice replacer (especially for picky eaters). In our pre-Paleo days, my husband often enjoyed a bowl of white rice smothered with butter and soy sauce. Though that is definitely not my idea of a tasty meal, this recipe has given him a little taste of his past.

1. Rinse and remove the green leaves and stems from the cauliflower.
2. Cut the cauliflower into pieces that will fit into the mouth of your food processor.
3. Using your shred blade attachment, shred the cauliflower in the food processor.
4. Melt the butter or oil in a large skillet on medium heat.
5. Add the cauliflower, and cook for eight to ten minutes, stirring often to avoid burning.

Note:

This side goes great with the mild chicken curry or with gluten free tamari.

Recipe Notes

SIDE
DISHES

Cauliflower Fried Rice

Serves: 4

Prep Time: 10 minutes

Cook Time: 10 minutes

1 head cauliflower

1 cup mushrooms, sliced

½ cup onions, sliced

1 cup celery, sliced

2 tablespoons butter or coconut oil

As a child, my mother made fried rice as a way to use leftovers and extra veggies in the fridge. Sometimes, she also added leftover chicken, pork, and even beef. This recipe is a version of my mother's fried rice that I grew up loving. Feel free to put your own spin on this dish, and use whatever vegetables you enjoy most.

1. Rinse and remove the green leaves and stems from the cauliflower.

2. Cut the cauliflower into pieces that will fit into the mouth of your food processor.

3. Using your shred blade attachment, shred the cauliflower in the food processor.

4. Slice the mushrooms and dice the celery and onion, then set aside.

5. Melt the oil in a large skillet over medium heat.

6. Add the cauliflower, mushrooms, onions, and celery, and cook for eight to ten minutes, stirring often to avoid burning.

Recipe Notes

Serves: 4

Prep Time: 5 minutes

Cook Time: 15 minutes

3-4 pieces of bacon, chopped

1 small onion, chopped

10 ounces kale

Sautéed Kale, Onion, and Bacon

Kale is a big hit in our house, especially with Kayden. By adding bacon to this nutrient-dense vegetable, you can't go wrong. This side dish goes well with just about any meal, slow cooked or not.

1. In a large skillet, chop the bacon into bite-sized pieces, and sauté it with the onion over medium heat until the onions are translucent.

2. Add the kale, and sauté until the bacon is thoroughly cooked and the kale is tender (about eight to ten minutes).

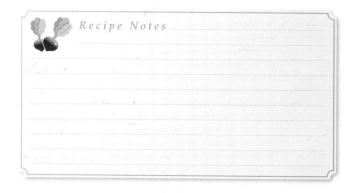

Recipe Notes

Serves: 4

Prep Time: 5 minutes

Cook Time: 5 minutes

½ cup honey

2 cups organic ketchup

¼ cup liquid smoke

¼ cup prepared mustard

1 tablespoon allspice

½ tablespoon cayenne pepper

Grandpa's BBQ Sauce

This recipe takes me back to my childhood. My grandfather was notorious for mixing and matching all kinds of crazy concoctions, and this sauce was one of my all-time favorites. It's so versatile that you can use it as a dipping sauce for my Beef Brisket, BBQ chicken, tasty pulled pork, or Grandpa's BBQ Beef.

1. Combine all ingredients in a large sauce pan.
2. Simmer and stir often for about five minutes.

Recipe Notes

Serves: 4-6

Prep Time: 8 minutes

Cook Time: none

Fresh spinach leaves

¼ sweet purple onion

2 mandarin oranges

Dried cranberries and walnuts

Citrus Spinach Salad

This salad is simple, yet refreshing. The mandarin oranges, cranberries, and walnuts add a sweet taste and a texture that will leave you wanting more. Feel free to add your choice of meat, like grilled steak or chicken.

1. Wash the spinach leaves, and place them in a large bowl.

2. Thinly slice the onion, and place it on top of the spinach.

3. Peel and separate the mandarin orange segments, and add them to the salad.

4. Sprinkle dried cranberries and walnuts to your liking, and top the salad with your favorite dressing.

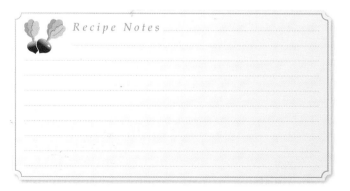

Recipe Notes

- large skillet
- measuring cup
- measuring spoon
- cutting board
- knife

Serves: 3-5

Prep Time: 20 minutes

Cook Time: 15 minutes

¼ cup coconut oil

1 small yellow onion, sliced

½ cup chopped walnuts

1 large bunch chard, stalks cut into bite-sized pieces and leaves removed

½ tablespoon balsamic vinegar

¼ cup dried cranberries

Sea salt and black pepper to taste

Caramelized Onion and Chard Salad

If you haven't figured out a way to enjoy your greens, this salad is sure to convince you that these healthy veggies can be delicious. The key is the caramelized onions. The first time I made this dish, it almost didn't make it to the dinner table; it was so good that I wanted to keep it all for myself. I'll bet even your kiddos will give this greens dish a nod of approval!

1. In a large skillet, heat the coconut oil over medium heat.

2. Add the sliced onions, and sauté them until the onions are caramelized.

3. Add the chopped walnuts, and sauté for another three to four minutes.

4. Add the chard and cranberries, and cook until the chard is wilted. Remove from heat.

5. Add the balsamic vinegar, salt and pepper, and stir well.

6. Serve immediately.

Recipe Notes

Serves: 4-6

Prep Time: 15 minutes

Cook Time: 10-12 minutes

1 bunch fresh kale or bag of pre-washed and cut kale from Trader Joe's

Olive oil

Balsamic vinegar

Salt to taste

Kayden's Kale Chips

This is one of Kayden's favorite things to help me make and eat. Kids really do make the best helpers in the kitchen (even if it means things take a little longer to prepare or requires little extra clean up). I don't specify amounts for the olive oil or balsamic vinegar because you can't go wrong with this recipe. The more you use, the tangier it will be, so season to your liking. These kale chips make a great side to any dish and are best enjoyed right out of the oven.

1. Pull kale leaves from the stems, and place the leaves in a large bowl. Repeat for each leaf of kale.

2. Rinse the kale well under cool water, and lay the leaves on a towel, patting them dry. Or spin them dry in a salad spinner.

3. Preheat oven to 350°F.

4. Return the kale to a large bowl, and drizzle it with olive oil and balsamic vinegar. Mix well to ensure that all of the kale has been coated.

5. Line a baking sheet with aluminum foil (makes for easy cleanup), and carefully lay the kale on the baking sheet so that none of it is touching.

6. Bake at 350°F for ten to twelve minutes or just until crisp. Salt them to taste. (Be sure to watch, as these will burn quickly.)

Note:

You can also substitute fresh squeezed lemon juice for the balsamic vinegar for an even zestier taste.

Recipe Notes

Serves: 4-6

Prep Time: 10 minutes

Cook Time: 15-20 minutes

1 pound Brussels sprouts

Olive oil

Salt and pepper to taste

Roasted Brussels Sprouts

Most people either love or hate Brussels sprouts. I remember not liking them myself as a child, but they have now become a staple vegetable in our house. Kayden loves the crispy chip-like pieces that separate during the cooking process. I think it is his fun excuse to be a cave boy and eat with his hands.

1. Wash and cut the stems off of the Brussels sprouts. Slice each in half, and place them in an oven-safe baking dish. (I use a 13x9 glass dish.)

2. Drizzle them with olive oil, salt, and pepper. Mix well to ensure that all of the Brussels sprouts are evenly coated.

3. Bake at 350°F for fifteen to twenty minutes or until they have reached the desired crispness.

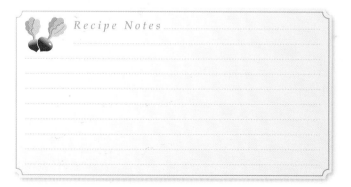

Recipe Notes

Tools:

- cutting board
- knife
- measuring cup
- large bowl

Serves: 4-6

Prep Time: 10 minutes

Cook Time: none

1 fresh pineapple, cored, peeled, and chopped

1 fresh mango, peeled and chopped

1 small jicama, peeled and chopped

¼ cup diced cilantro

Juice of 1 lime

Pineapple Mango Jicama Salsa

This side dish is sweet and cool, and it's sure to be a hit at your summer BBQ or potluck gathering. It can be enjoyed as a side to virtually any dish or even goes well on top of chicken or pork.

1. Cut the top and bottom off of the pineapple about a half of an inch from the top and bottom.

2. Stand the pineapple on its end, and use a long knife to cut away the rugged skin. Repeat until the entire pineapple is peeled.

3. Cut the peeled pineapple into quarters lengthwise, and remove the tough core.

4. Chop the cored and peeled pineapple into bite-sized chunks, and place the pieces in a large bowl.

5. Peel, slice, and chop the mango and jicama into bite-sized chunks, and place them in the bowl with the pineapple.

6. Add the cilantro and lime juice, mix well, and serve.

Recipe Notes

Salsa Verde

Tools:

- large soup pot
- cutting board
- knife
- food processor or blender

Serves: 4-6

Prep Time: 15 minutes

Cook Time: 15 minutes

8-10 tomatillos, shucked

2 jalapeño peppers

3-4 serrano peppers

2 cloves garlic

½ cup cilantro

2 green onions, diced (optional)

Juice of 1 lime

Salt to taste

I feel very privileged to have grown up with a culturally diverse extended family. Our holiday gatherings usually consisted of a smoked turkey, lasagna, rice pilaf, enchiladas, chile rellenos, and one or two salsas. This version is my favorite salsa verde. Not only is this recipe relatively quick to make, it is also easy to dictate the "heat" or spiciness. My family prefers a spicy salsa, but you can make it milder by adding extra tomato and omitting the seeds from the peppers.

1. Shuck and rinse the tomatillos by running warm water over them and peeling back the husks. Set them aside.

2. Fill a large soup pot half to three-quarters full of water, and place the tomatillos (husks removed), jalapeños, and serranos in the pot.

3. Bring the pot of water to a slow boil. Remove it from the heat when the tomatillos start to turn a lighter shade of green or are soft to the touch. (Be careful not to burn yourself, as they will be hot.)

4. Remove the tomatillos and peppers from the water, and place them in a food processor or blender along with the garlic and cilantro. Pulse until it reaches a smooth salsa consistency.

5. Pour the mixture into a serving bowl.

6. If using onions, dice the onions, and add them to the salsa.

7. Squeeze the lime juice into the salsa, and salt it to taste.

Recipe Notes

Serves: 4

Prep Time: 5 minutes

Cook Time: 8-10 minutes

1 bunch spinach, washed

2 tablespoons olive oil or coconut oil

1-2 cloves garlic, crushed

Salt and pepper to taste

Garlic Spinach

When I was a kid, I despised spinach. As an adult, I revisited this old family staple. Instead of steaming the spinach, I sautéed it with a little garlic, and the result was far from what I remembered as a child. By sautéing it, you can control how "done" you want your spinach. I like to remove it from the heat as soon as the leaves turn dark green. This recipe is great topped with my Spaghetti Sauce (page 114) or as a side to my morning eggs.

1. Wash the spinach leaves, and either pat them dry with towels or spin dry them using a salad spinner.

2. Place the olive oil or coconut oil in a large skillet over medium-low heat.

3. Using a garlic crusher, crush the garlic into the skillet.

4. Add the spinach to the skillet, and sauté over medium-low heat until the spinach leaves turn dark green.

5. Remove from heat immediately to avoid over-cooking. Add salt and pepper to taste.

Recipe Notes

Slow Cooked Sweet Potatoes

Serves: 4-6

Prep Time: 5 minutes

Cook Time: 6-8 hours on low

6-10 sweet potatoes, rinsed

This side dish is designed for bachelors. I like to make my sweet potatoes like this if I know I'm planning other meals that involve sweet potato like my Jalapeño Sweet Potato Chowder or even if I just have a crazy week ahead of me. It's nice to have one less thing to cook when I'm busy. Like Top Ramen, it is hard to mess this up; you just put the sweet potatoes in the slow cooker and turn it on.

1. Rinse the sweet potatoes, and place them in the slow cooker. It is okay to stack them on top of each other.

2. Cover, and cook on low for six to eight hours. To avoid having the sweet potatoes on the bottom split open, rotate them halfway through the cooking process.

Recipe Notes

Serves: 4-6

Prep Time: 10 minutes

Cook Time: 15-20 minutes

2 large sweet potatoes

¼ cup coconut oil

Salt to taste

Sweet Potato Chips

Chips don't have to be a thing of the past. We have found that cooking a sweet potato this way makes for a great chip and even a bread substitute. I have to give my picky husband credit for this, as years ago, he is the one who gave me this idea. Since then, we have enjoyed our hamburgers sandwiched between two large and crispy sweet potatoes. They're a much healthier alternative to regular chips, bread, or French fries. And even kids will enjoy them.

1. Place the coconut oil in a large skillet, and melt it over medium-high heat.

2. Peel and slice the sweet potatoes. If you are using the sweet potatoes as your bun/bread for a sandwich or burger, slice them thinly lengthwise. If you are enjoying them as a snack, slice them thinly into rounds.

3. Place an even layer of the sliced sweet potatoes into the hot skillet. Cook until golden brown (about three minutes), flipping each wheel with tongs and cooking for another three minutes or until golden brown.

4. Remove the chips from the skillet, and place them on paper towels on a plate.

5. Repeat until all chips have been cooked.

6. Salt to taste.

Recipe Notes

Serves: 4

Prep Time: 8 minutes

Cook Time: none

1 head green cabbage, rinsed and chopped

½ bunch of cilantro

Salad dressing of your choice (optional)

- Serves well with-

Mild Shredded Chicken page 124

Grandpa's BBQ Beef page 136

NorCal Margarita Chicken page 146

Simple Cabbage and Cilantro Salad

This is another ridiculously easy side dish that pairs well with so many other dishes, such as the NorCal Margarita Chicken. You can also enjoy it by itself or top it with pulled beef or pork.

1. Peel off and discard the outer layer of the cabbage. Chop the cabbage into bite-sized pieces, and place it in a colander or salad spinner.

2. Rinse and drain the cabbage, and place it in a large salad or serving bowl.

3. Rinse and chop the cilantro, and add it on top of the cabbage.

4. Mix the cabbage and cilantro well, and top with your favorite salad dressing.

Recipe Notes

Grilled Asparagus

Serves: 4

Prep Time: 5 minutes

Cook Time: 10 minutes

1 bunch asparagus, rinsed

Olive oil

Salt and garlic pepper to taste

My father is the grill master in the family. I think it would be fair to say that he would attempt to grill just about anything and everything. One of my summertime favorites is grilled veggies. Asparagus is easy to grill and doesn't require any extra apparatus.

1. Rinse off the asparagus, cutting or snapping off the ends of the stalks.

2. Place the asparagus on a plate.

3. Drizzle it with olive oil, and sprinkle with garlic pepper and salt.

4. Place the asparagus perpendicular on a preheated grill over medium heat, so that they will not fall through the grill cracks. Grill until the asparagus starts to turn golden and crisp, rotating often.

Recipe Notes

SIDE
DISHES

Broccoli Sauté

Tools:
- cutting board
- knife
- large skillet

Serves: 4-6

Prep Time: 5 minutes

Cook Time: 15 minutes

3 cups broccoli florets, rinsed

2 cloves garlic, minced

2 tablespoons olive oil or coconut oil

This side dish is a nice twist on traditional steamed broccoli. In the past, I have been known to over-steam my broccoli, so sautéing it provides a tender, yet crisp, side dish. I love to eat this broccoli with my Red Beef Curry (page 138), although you can even serve it with a traditional BBQ meal.

1. Place the olive oil or coconut oil in a large skillet, and heat it over medium heat.

2. Mince the garlic, and add it to the oil in the skillet.

3. Add the broccoli florets to the garlic and oil, and sauté over medium heat for about 15 minutes or until broccoli is just tender.

Recipe Notes

· large soup pot	· garlic crusher
· measuring spoons	· hand mixer or potato masher
· measuring cup	

Serves: 4-6

Prep Time: 5 minutes

Cook Time: 20 minutes

4-5 yellow sweet potatoes, peeled and chopped

1-2 tablespoons butter or ghee (optional)

2 cloves garlic, crushed

2-3 tablespoons green onion or scallions, diced

¼ cup chicken stock

Garlic Mashed Sweet Potatoes

Mashed potatoes make an appearance at every family event on my mother's side of the family. It's a classic staple for many families, I'm sure! After changing our family's eating habits, I wanted to create a side dish that was a happy medium for both myself and my husband, while still taking us back to those family gatherings that are so dear to my heart.

1. Fill a large soup pot half to three-quarters of the way full with water, and bring it to a slow boil.

2. Peel and chop the sweet potatoes, and add them to the boiling water. Boil for ten to twelve minutes or until the sweet potatoes are tender when poked with a fork.

3. Drain the water from the sweet potatoes, and place them in a large serving bowl.

4. In a small saucepan, sauté the garlic and onions in the butter over medium heat for two to three minutes.

5. Pour the butter mixture over the sweet potatoes in the bowl.

6. Using a potato masher or hand mixer, beat the sweet potatoes and butter until smooth.

7. Add the chicken stock to the mixture slowly until you reached the desired consistency.

Recipe Notes

Serves: 4

Prep Time: 10 minutes

Cook Time: none

3-4 ripe avocados, sliced and chunked

¼ cup daikon radish, diced

Juice of 1 lime

Cilantro for garnish

Salt to taste

Avocado Salsa

This mild salsa tastes great on top of almost any dish. My favorites are Fiesta Lime Chicken (page 176) or Carne Asada (page 156). If you have a spicier palate, add a little Salsa Verde (page 200) to this Avocado Salsa recipe.

1. Cut the avocados in half lengthwise, and remove the seeds. Using an avocado slicer (or knife), cut the avocados into long slices, and place them in a medium-sized serving bowl.

2. Then, cut the avocados into chunks by cutting across the slices.

3. Peel and dice the daikon radish, and add it to the avocado chunks.

4. Squeeze the lime juice over the avocado and daikon, and garnish with the cilantro.

5. Add salt to taste.

6. Give the mixture a few good stirs to ensure that the lime and salt are evenly dispersed.

Recipe Notes

Cucumber Salad

Tools:
- peeler
- cutting board
- knife
- large bowl

Serves: 4

Prep Time: 10 minutes

Cook Time: none

2 large cucumbers, peeled and chopped

2 tomatoes, sliced into wedges

½ purple onion, sliced

Salt and pepper to taste

This is one of my favorite salads to make in the summer. I enjoy going to the local farmers' market and picking up these fresh ingredients. You can enjoy this salad as is with a little salt and pepper or dress it up with balsamic vinegar and olive oil.

1. Peel the cucumber, and then quarter and chop it into bite-sized pieces. Place the pieces in a large serving bowl.

2. Slice the tomatoes into wedges, and place them in the bowl with the cucumber pieces.

3. Cut one end off of the onion, and peel and discard the outer layer. Finely slice half of the onion into rings, and add the onion to the serving bowl. (You may need to separate the onion slices into rings with your hands as you add them to the bowl.)

4. Add salt and pepper to taste.

Recipe Notes

Spaghetti Squash

Tools:

· cutting board
· knife
· spoon
· oven safe dish

Serves: 4-6

Prep Time: 10 minutes

Cook Time: 40-60 minutes

1 spaghetti squash

Spaghetti squash has the closest resemblance to pasta. You can enjoy this side dish served with my Spaghetti Sauce (page 114) or Pesto (page 68). My husband even eats it as is with just a dab of butter.

1. Cut the spaghetti squash in half lengthwise. Using a spoon, scoop out and discard the seeds.

2. Place the two halves of spaghetti squash in an oven-safe dish (I use a glass Pyrex dish) face down.

3. Fill the dish halfway with water, and place it in the oven. Bake at 350°F for forty minutes to an hour or until the squash is easily pulled from the sides.

Note:

*You can also prepare your squash in the microwave.
Though it is not my preferred method, it can be done
in a matter of minutes. Simply follow the above instructions,
but place the squash in a microwave dish, cooking on high
for eight to ten minutes.*

Recipe Notes

Serves: 4

Prep Time: 5 minutes

Cook Time: 6 hours on low

3 medium sweet potatoes

1 medium apple

1 tablespoon cinnamon

Robb's Post Workout Carbaganza!

Post-workout carbohydrate repletion can be as easy as it is tasty. This recipe is perfect for the hard-training athlete who wants a quick and tasty post-workout carb bomb.

1. Wash and peel the sweet potatoes, and place them in the slow cooker.

2. Wash, cut, core, and peel the apple. Add it over the sweet potatoes.

3. Add the cinnamon to the apple and sweet potato mixture.

4. Cover and cook on low for six hours or until soft.

5. Place the sweet potato, apple, and cinnamon mixture in a blender or food processor, and purée until smooth. Alternatively, use a potato masher for a slightly thicker consistency.

6. Add additional cinnamon to taste.

7. Eat warm, or chill for later.

Recipe Notes

DESSERTS

Banana Bread

Tools:

- large mixing bowl
- fork
- measuring spoons
- measuring cups
- parchment paper

Serves: 6-8

Prep Time: 10 minutes

Cook Time: 2 hours on low

4 small ripe bananas

¼ cup + 2 tablespoons melted coconut oil

½ cup honey

1 tablespoon vanilla

3 tablespoons coconut milk

3 eggs

2 cups almond flour

1 teaspoon baking soda

You might wonder, "Why make Banana Bread in a slow cooker when you can just as easily make it in the oven?" Making it in the slow cooker keeps it warm and moist much longer. It also travels well right in the slow cooker, making it easy to take along to parties or potlucks, where it's always a big hit. Wouldn't you like to be able to have warm banana bread even hours after it has finished cooking? It's one of my husband's absolute favorites!

1. In a large mixing bowl, mash the four ripe bananas with a fork.

2. Add the melted coconut oil to the bowl.

3. Stir in the honey, vanilla, coconut milk, and eggs. Mix well.

4. Add the flour and baking soda. The mixture will be thin, like pancake batter.

5. Line your slow cooker with parchment paper (see tip on page 60).

6. Pour the banana mixture into the slow cooker, and cook on low for two hours.

7. When the bread is done, you can either remove it by carefully lifting the parchment paper out and placing the banana bread on a cutting board, or you can simply leave it in the slow cooker on the warm setting to enjoy warm banana bread throughout the day.

Recipe Notes

DESSERT

Tempting Chocolate Cake

Tools:
- parchment paper
- spoon
- medium and large bowl
- measuring cups
- measuring spoons

Serves: 6-8

Prep Time: 15 minutes

Cook Time: 1½ to 2 hours on low

¾ cup + 3 tablespoons of almond flour (preferably blanched)

3 tablespoons unsweetened cocoa powder

2 teaspoons baking powder

½ cup honey

¾ cup melted butter, ghee, or coconut oil

1 tablespoon vanilla

¾ cup high fat coconut milk

3 eggs

¼ cup dark chocolate chips

This cake will satisfy the craving of every dark chocolate lover out there. With its light and moist consistency and rich dark chocolate flavor, this is sure to be a holiday hit for even the non-Paleo guest. What I love most about this cake is how easy it is to make! I used to spend hours in the kitchen trying to bake for special occasions. Not anymore!

1. Line the inside of the slow cooker with parchment paper (see tip on page 60).

2. In a medium-sized bowl, combine the almond flour, cocoa powder, and baking powder, and set aside.

3. In a large separate bowl, stir the honey and melted butter or ghee together.

4. Add 1 tablespoon of vanilla to the butter and honey mixture.

5. Stir the coconut milk into the vanilla, butter, and honey mixture.

6. Add the three eggs to the wet mixture. Be sure that the mixture is cool before adding the eggs to avoid prematurely cooking them.

7. Combine the dry ingredients to the wet ingredients, and mix well. It should have a soup-like consistency.

8. Stir in the chocolate chips.

9. Pour the mixture into the slow cooker, and cook on low for approximately two hours.

Recipe Notes

DESSERT

Tools:

- large and small mixing bowl
- knife
- parchment paper
- measuring cups
- measuring spoon

Serves: 6-8

Prep Time: 10-15 minutes

Cook Time: 1½ hours on low

¾ cup almond flour

½ cup unsweetened cocoa powder

¾ teaspoon baking powder

¼ cup + 2 tablespoons melted coconut oil

½ cup honey

1 tablespoon vanilla

3 eggs

¼ cup dark chocolate chips

3 tablespoons Ammin Nut Chunky Almond Butter or almond butter of your choice

Chocolate Almond Butter Swirl Brownies

This tasty treat was inspired by our friends at Ammin Nut Company. I wanted to make something that resembled an old pre-Paleo favorite—a brownie with the rich, dark flavor of chocolate and a hint of peanut butter. So, I went to work and came up with this brownie with just a swirl of almond butter instead of the standard peanut butter. Truly delectable, and even better than my old favorite! It is hands down one of Kayden's favorite treats. Keep in mind that this is definitely a treat, but worth the indulgence for that special occasion.

1. In a small bowl, combine the almond flour, cocoa powder, and baking powder.
2. In a separate bowl, combine the melted coconut oil and honey, and stir well.
3. Add the vanilla to the wet ingredients.
4. When the coconut oil has cooled, add the eggs.
5. Combine the wet and dry mixtures, stirring well.
6. Add the dark chocolate chips.
7. Line your slow cooker with parchment paper (see tip on page 60), and add the brownie mixture.
8. Drop the almond butter on top of the brownie mixture. (You can use more if you want.)
9. Using a knife, swirl the almond butter throughout the brownie mixture.
10. Place the lid on the slow cooker, and cook on low for one and one-quarter hours.

Note:

*You can also bake these in the oven.
To do so, follow the above instructions, but pour the batter into an 8x8 glass baking dish greased with coconut oil.
Bake for 20 minutes at 350°F.*

DESSERT

 *Recipe Notes*

Tools:

- peeler
- small bowl
- knife
- cutting board
- measuring spoon
- measuring cup

Serves: 4

Prep Time: 10 minutes

Cook Time: 2 hours on low

4-6 Gala apples

1 tablespoon cinnamon

1 tablespoon butter, ghee, or coconut oil

- Topping -

2 tablespoons melted butter, ghee, or coconut oil

1 cup almond flour

1 tablespoon honey

Apple Crumble

This dessert reminds me of the apple pie my family had at Thanksgiving, but much better! What I appreciate about eating Paleo is that I can now enjoy the sweetness of fruit on its own without relying on sugar-filled desserts. This recipe is sweetened only by one tablespoon of honey and the natural flavor of ripe apples.

1. Peel, core, and chop the apples into small bite-sized pieces, and place them in your slow cooker.

2. Add the cinnamon, and mix until all the apple slices are coated with it.

3. Dot the apple and cinnamon mixture with one tablespoon of butter.

4. For the topping, melt two tablespoons of butter in a small bowl. Stir the almond flour into the melted butter, and add the honey. Mix together until it starts to crumble.

5. Sprinkle the topping mixture evenly over the apples in the slow cooker. Cook on low for two hours.

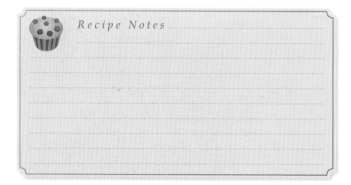
Recipe Notes

Serves: 4-6

Prep Time: 5 minutes

Cook Time: 2 hours on low

3-4 cups fresh or frozen mixed berries (blackberries, raspberries, and strawberries work great)

1 tablespoon butter (optional)

- *Topping* -

2 tablespoons melted butter, ghee, or coconut oil

1 cup almond flour

1 tablespoon honey

DESSERT

Berry Crumble

This recipe is similar to the apple crumble, but made with berries instead. My favorite time of year for this recipe is during our hot Chico summers when blackberries are at their ripest. We even have several wild blackberry bushes growing throughout our parks, so we can always count on our local farmers' markets to have baskets of delicious berries. Fortunately, this crumble also turns out yummy using frozen berries, so you can enjoy this treat any time of year.

1. Place the berries in your slow cooker, dot with butter if you choose.

2. For the topping, melt two tablespoons of butter in a small bowl. Stir the almond flour into the melted butter, and add the honey. Mix together until it starts to crumble.

3. Sprinkle the topping mixture evenly over the berries in the slow cooker. Cook on low for two hours.

Recipe Notes

Spice Blends

Makes approx. 2 Tablespoons

Chico Rub

1 teaspoon pepper

1½ teaspoon paprika

1 teaspoon sage

1 ½ teaspoon allspice

1 teaspoon basil

Fiery Sunset

1¼ teaspoon ground ancho chili pepper

1¼ teaspoon onion powder

1¼ teaspoon garlic powder

1¼ teaspoon ground chipotle pepper

1 teaspoon cocoa powder

pinch of red pepper (optional)

Garden Rae

1 ½ teaspoon thyme

1 ½ teaspoon basil

1 ½ teaspoon garlic powder

1 ½ teaspoon onion powder

Kicking Chili

1¼ teaspoon ground ancho chili pepper

¾ teaspoon cumin

¾ teaspoon garlic powder

½ teaspoon onion powder

¾ teaspoon paprika

¾ teaspoon oregano

¾ teaspoon turmeric

½ teaspoon allspice

¼ teaspoon chili powder

Summer Blaze

2¾ teaspoon paprika

1½ teaspoon mustard

1½ teaspoon allspice

¼ teaspoon garlic powder

Cobblestone

1½ teaspoon paprika

¾ teaspoon celery salt

¾ teaspoon garlic powder

¾ teaspoon onion powder

¾ teaspoon turmeric

¾ teaspoon basil

¼ teaspoon rosemary

¼ teaspoon thyme

Penzeys Spices

I love Penzeys spices! If I had more time, I would prefer to make my own spice blends, but that just isn't the case. Penzeys offers a variety of spice blends, as well as individual spices and herbs. What I love most is that all of the ingredients are listed on the jars/bags, as well as online, so I know exactly what I'm getting. Visit www.penzeys.com

INGREDIENT INDEX

Penzeys California Pepper, 130
Penzeys Chili 9000, 132
Penzeys Galena Street Rib and Chicken Rub Spice, 80, 86, 112
Penzeys Mural of Flavor, 82, 102, 104
Penzeys Old World Seasoning, 116
Pesto, 68, 120
pineapple, 112, 126, 198
pineapple juice, 126
poblano peppers, 122
pork, 112, 122, 126, 142, 144, 148, 150, 158, 162, 166
pork loin chops, 144
pork loins, 148
pork shoulder, 122
portobello mushrooms, 92

-r-
radish, 216
red chili pepper, 112, 132
red curry paste, 138
red pepper flakes, 86, 138
red wine vinegar, 106
ribs, 112, 122, 150, 172
rice vinegar, 92, 168
rosemary, 148, 152

-s-
sage, 66, 152
sausage, 60, 64, 66, 114, 134, 142, 162
scallions, 214
serrano peppers, 122, 132, 200
sesame oil, 92
sesame seed oil, 168
shallots, 82

short ribs, 172
shrimp, 160
spaghetti squash, 220
spinach, 60, 82, 162, 190, 202
stew meat, 88, 106
sweet potato, 60, 62, 64, 66, 82, 84, 88, 118, 204, 206, 214, 222

-t-
tequila, 146
thyme, 88, 90, 152
tomatillos, 122, 132, 200
tomato paste, 110, 130, 132
tomato sauce, 80, 128, 130, 158, 172, 174
tomatoes, 68, 80, 82, 86, 88, 90, 94, 96, 106, 114, 128, 132, 134, 160, 166, 178, 218
Trader Joe's taco seasoning, 176
turkey breast, 152
turnip, 80

-v-
vanilla, 226, 228, 230
vegetable broth, 82
vegetable stock, 140

-w-
walnut oil, 68, 120
walnuts, 190, 192
water chestnuts, 92, 168
wheat-free tamari, 92, 168
white wine, 128
winter squash, 80
Worcestershire sauce, 140

-y-
yam, 60, 62, 64
yellow curry, 118

-z-
zucchini, 68, 82, 114, 134, 160
zucchini squash, 68, 82